True
Revival
The Church's Greatest Need

This book was
Cover designed by David Berthiaume
Cover art © iStockphoto.com
Typeset: Bembo 11.5/14

PRINTED IN U.S.A.

14   13   12   11   5   4   3

Third Printing

Library of Congress Cataloging-in-Publication Data
White, Ellen Gould Harmon, 1827-1915.
  True revival : the church's greatest need : selections from the writings
of Ellen G. White.
      p. cm.
  1. Christian life--Seventh-Day Adventist authors. 2. Revivals. I. Title.
  BV4501.3.W463 2010
  248.4'86732--dc22

                                    2010041578

ISBN 978-0-8280-2572-0

True
Revival

The Church's Greatest Need

Selections from the writings of

ELLEN G. WHITE

REVIEW AND HERALD® PUBLISHING ASSOCIATION
Since 1861 | www.reviewandherald.com

To order additional copies of
True Revival, or other books by Ellen G. White,
call **1-800-765-6955**.

Visit us at
www.reviewandherald.com
for information on other Review and Herald® products.

Table of Contents

Preface

Why this book on revival and its fruitage? Many today have a hunger for something more than just "playing church" and going through the motions of the Christian life. They want a genuine experience with Christ—for themselves and for the church.

In these pages you will find Ellen G. White addressing these longings, pointing the way to that deeper experience and warning of some pitfalls along the way. She shows that God is calling those who say they are followers of Jesus Christ to forsake the ways of the world and to recommit their lives to Him. It is time for a genuine revival and reformation in God's church. There is a work to be done, a world to be warned of its coming end.

This can happen only under the power of God's Spirit, and God's Spirit cannot be given to those who profess to be His people until they know by experience what repentance and reformation is. Ellen G. White wrote, "The Spirit and power of God will be poured out upon His children" (*True Revival,* p. 19). But it is the responsibility of His children to seek this gift. According to Ellen White, "the descent of the Holy Spirit upon the church is looked forward to as in the future; but it is the privilege of the church to have it now. Seek for it, pray for it, believe for it. We must have it, and Heaven is waiting to bestow it" (*Evangelism,* p. 701).

Being born again, justified, converted—this is the beginning. But what about growing up into Christ? What about that lifetime experience we sometimes call sanctification? Truly born-again Christians not only talk about Christ but live lives that testify that they are, in fact, followers of the Lord Jesus Christ. Revival is being born again; reformation is living a life of obedience through the

7

power of the Holy Spirit, the Spirit that "Heaven is waiting to bestow."

The Spirit-filled life results not only in personal victory over sin but also in a fresh desire and ability to share the Christian life and hope with others. Filled with the power of the Holy Spirit, God's faithful ones will proclaim the final message that will prepare a people for the Lord's return. Satan will do everything in his power to stop it. He will try to convince us that there are shortcuts—easier ways to have the fellowship with God that leads to an empowered Christian life. He will introduce counterfeits for the power of the Spirit—counterfeits so deceptive that if God's people do not maintain a deep, living relationship with Him, based on the Word of God, they will be deceived. This book will, among other things, help the reader to distinguish between the true and the false.

For more than 100 years Ellen White's much-loved book *Steps to Christ* has been a best seller. Young and old have accepted its appeal for commitment to Christ. For many, *True Revival: The Church's Greatest Need* will serve as a companion book, offering further guidance toward a life of genuine revival and renewal. Chapters 2-8 are taken from the little book *A New Life* (originally published as *Revival and Beyond)*, and chapters 1, 9, and 10 are taken from several chapters on revival and reformation in *Selected Messages*, book 1, pages 121-152.

In these closing moments of earth's sinful history, surely God's Holy Spirit is ready to give us the power to finish our work for others and the work necessary for ourselves. Can it be that you will be one through whom God will do something special? May this book help you to experience the revival and reformation that will prepare you for the latter rain and the soon return of our Lord.

The Trustees of the Ellen G. White Estate

Chapter 1:

Calls for a Revival

The Church's Greatest Need

A revival of true godliness among us is the greatest and most urgent of all our needs. To seek this should be our first work. There must be earnest effort to obtain the blessing of the Lord, not because God is not willing to bestow His blessing upon us, but because we are unprepared to receive it. Our heavenly Father is more willing to give His Holy Spirit to them that ask Him, than are earthly parents to give good gifts to their children. But it is our work, by confession, humiliation, repentance, and earnest prayer, to fulfill the conditions upon which God has promised to grant us His blessing. A revival need be expected only in answer to prayer. While the people are so destitute of God's Holy spirit, they cannot appreciate the preaching of the Word; but when the Spirit's power touches their hearts, then the discourses given will not be without effect. Guided by the teachings of God's Word, with the manifestation of His Spirit, in the exercise of sound discretion, those who attend our meetings will gain a precious experience, and returning home, will be prepared to exert a healthful influence.

The old standard bearers knew what it was to wrestle with God in prayer, and to enjoy the outpouring of His Spirit. But these are passing off from the stage of action; and who are coming up to fill their places? How is it with the rising generation? Are they converted to God? Are we awake to the work that is going on in the heavenly sanctuary, or are we waiting for some compelling power to come upon the church before we shall arouse? Are we hoping to see the whole church revived? That time will never come.

There are persons in the church who are not converted, and who will not unite in earnest, prevailing prayer. We must enter upon the work individually. We must pray more, and talk less. Iniquity abounds, and the people must be taught not to be satisfied with a form of godliness without the spirit and power. If we are intent upon searching our own hearts, putting away our sins, and correcting our evil tendencies, our souls will not be lifted up unto vanity; we shall be distrustful of ourselves, having an abiding sense that our sufficiency is of God.

We have far more to fear from within than from without. The hindrances to strength and success are far greater from the church itself than from the world. Unbelievers have a right to expect that those who profess to be keeping the commandments of God and the faith of Jesus, will do more than any other class to promote and honor, by their consistent lives, by their godly example and their active influence, the cause which they represent. But how often have the professed advocates of the truth proved the greatest obstacle to its advancement! The unbelief indulged, the doubts expressed, the darkness cherished, encourage the presence of evil angels, and open the way for the accomplishment of Satan's devices.

Opening the Door to the Adversary

The adversary of souls is not permitted to read the thoughts of men; but he is a keen observer, and he marks the words; he takes account of actions, and skillfully adapts his temptations to meet the cases of those who place themselves in his power. If we would labor to repress sinful thoughts and feelings, giving them no expression in words or actions, Satan would be defeated; for he could not prepare his specious temptations to meet the case.

But how often do professed Christians, by their lack of self-control, open the door to the adversary of souls! Divisions, and even bitter dissensions which would disgrace any worldly community, are common in the churches, because there is so little effort to control wrong feelings, and to repress every word that Satan can take advantage of. As soon as an alienation of feeling arises, the matter is spread before Satan for his inspection, and the opportunity given for him to use his serpentlike wisdom and skill in dividing and destroying the church. There is great loss in every dissension. Personal friends of both parties take sides with their respective favorites, and thus the breach is widened. A house divided against itself cannot stand. Criminations and recriminations are engendered and multiplied. Satan and his angels are actively at work to secure a harvest from seed thus sown.

Worldlings look on, and jeeringly exclaim, "Behold how these Christians hate one another! If this is religion, we do not want it." And they look upon themselves and their irreligious characters with great satisfaction. Thus they are confirmed in their impenitence, and Satan exults at his success.

The great deceiver has prepared his wiles for every soul that is not braced for trial and guarded by constant prayer and living faith. As ministers, as Christians, we must work to take the stumbling blocks out of the way. We must remove every obstacle. Let us confess and forsake every sin, that the way of the Lord may be prepared, that He may come into our assemblies and impart His rich grace. The world, the flesh, and the devil must be overcome.

We cannot prepare the way by gaining the friendship of the world, which is enmity with God; but by His help we can break its seductive influence upon ourselves and upon others. We cannot individually or as a body secure ourselves from the constant temptations of a relentless and determined foe; but in the strength of Jesus we can resist them.

From every member of the church a steady light may shine forth before the world, so that they shall not be led to inquire, What do these people more than others? There can be and must be a withdrawal from conformity to the world, a shunning of all appearance of evil, so that no occasion shall be given for gainsayers. We cannot escape reproach; it will come; but we should be very careful that we are not reproached for our own sins or follies, but for Christ's sake.

There is nothing that Satan fears so much as that the people of God shall clear the way by removing every hindrance, so that the Lord can pour out His Spirit upon a languishing church and an impenitent congregation. If Satan had his way, there would never be another awakening, great or small, to the end of time. But we are not ignorant of his devices. It is possible to resist his power. When the way is prepared for the Spirit of God, the blessing will come. Satan can no more hinder a shower of blessing from descending upon God's people than he can close the windows of heaven that rain cannot come upon the earth. Wicked men and devils cannot hinder the work of God, or shut out His presence from the assemblies of His people, if they will, with subdued, contrite hearts, confess and put away their sins, and in faith claim His promises. Every temptation, every opposing influence, whether open or secret, may be successfully resisted, "not by might, nor by power, but by my spirit, saith the Lord of hosts" (Zech. 4:6).

We Are in the Day of Atonement

We are in the great day of atonement, when our sins are, by confession and repentance, to go beforehand to judgment. God does not now accept a tame, spiritless testimony from His ministers. Such a testimony would not be present truth. The message for this time must be meat in due season to feed the church of God. But Satan has been seeking gradually to rob this message of its power, that the people may not be prepared to stand in the day of the Lord.

In 1844 our great High Priest entered the most holy place of the heavenly sanctuary, to begin the work of the investigative judgment. The cases of the righteous dead have been passing in review before God. When that work shall be completed, judgment is to be pronounced upon the living. How precious, how important are these solemn moments! Each of us has a case pending in the court of heaven. We are individually to be judged according to the deeds done in the body. In the typical service, when the work of atonement was performed by the high priest in the most holy place of the earthly sanctuary, the people were required to afflict their souls before God, and confess their sins, that they might be atoned for and blotted out. Will any less be required of us in this antitypical day of atonement, when Christ in the sanctuary above is pleading in behalf of His people, and the final, irrevocable decision is to be pronounced upon every case?

What is our condition in this fearful and solemn time? Alas, what pride is prevailing in the church, what hypocrisy, what deception, what love of dress, frivolity, and amusement, what desire for the supremacy! All these sins have clouded the mind, so that eternal things have not been discerned. Shall we not search the Scriptures, that we may know where we are in this world's history? Shall we not become intelligent in regard to the work that is being accomplished for us at this time, and the position that we as sinners should occupy while this work of atonement is going forward? If we have any regard for our souls' salvation, we must make a decided change. We must seek the Lord with true penitence; we must with deep contrition of soul confess our sins, that they may be blotted out.

We must no longer remain upon the enchanted ground. We are fast approaching the close of our probation. Let every soul inquire, How do I stand before God? We know not how soon our names may be taken into the lips of Christ, and our cases be finally decided. What, oh, what will these decisions be! Shall we be counted with the righteous, or shall we be numbered with the wicked?

The Church to Arise and Repent

Let the church arise, and repent of her backslidings before God. Let the watchmen awake, and give the trumpet a certain sound. It is a definite warning that we have to proclaim. God commands His servants, "Cry aloud, spare not, lift up thy voice like a trumpet, and shew my people their transgression, and the house of Jacob their sins" (Isa. 58:1). The attention of the people must be gained; unless this can be done, all effort is useless; though an angel from heaven should come down and speak to them, his words would do no more good than if he were speaking into the cold ear of death.

The church must arouse to action. The Spirit of God can never come in until she prepares the way. There should be earnest searching of heart. There should be united, persevering prayer, and through faith a claiming of the promises of God. There should be, not a clothing of the body with sackcloth, as in ancient times, but a deep humiliation of soul. We have not the first reason for self-congratulation and self-exaltation. We should humble ourselves under the mighty hand of God. He will appear to comfort and bless the true seekers.

The work is before us; will we engage in it? We must work fast, we must go steadily forward. We must be preparing for the great day of the Lord. We have no time to lose, no time to be engaged in selfish purposes. The world is to be warned. What are we doing as individuals to bring the light before others? God has left to every man his work; every one has a part to act, and we cannot neglect this work except at the peril of our souls.

O my brethren, will you grieve the Holy Spirit, and cause it to depart? Will you shut out the blessed Saviour, because you are unprepared for His presence? Will you leave souls to perish without the knowledge of the truth, because you love your ease too well to bear the burden that Jesus bore for you? Let us awake out of sleep. "Be sober, be vigilant; because your adversary the devil, as a roaring lion, walketh about, seeking whom he may devour" (1 Peter 5:8).—*The Review and Herald*, March 22, 1887.

Reformation Accompanies Revival

In many hearts there seems to be scarcely a breath of spiritual life. This makes me very sad. I fear that aggressive warfare against the world, the flesh, and the devil has not been maintained. Shall we cheer on, by a half-dead Christianity, the selfish, covetous spirit of the world, sharing its ungodliness and smiling on its falsehood?—Nay! By the grace of God let us be steadfast to the principles of truth, holding firm to the end the beginning of our confidence. We are to be "not slothful in business; fervent in spirit; serving the Lord" (Rom. 12:11). One is our Master, even Christ. To Him we are to look. From Him we are to receive our wisdom. By His grace we are to preserve our integrity, standing before God in meekness and contrition, and representing Him to the world.

Sermons have been in great demand in our churches. The members have depended upon pulpit declamations instead of on the Holy Spirit. Uncalled for and unused, the spiritual gifts bestowed on them have dwindled into feebleness. If the ministers would go forth into new fields, the members would be obliged to bear responsibilities, and by use their capabilities would increase.

God brings against ministers and people the heavy charge of spiritual feebleness, saying, "I know thy works, that thou art neither cold nor hot: I would thou wert cold or hot. So then because thou art lukewarm, and neither cold nor hot, I will spue thee out of my mouth. Because thou sayest, I am rich, and increased with goods, and have need of nothing; and knowest not that thou art wretched, and miserable, and poor, and blind, and naked: I counsel thee to buy of me gold tried in the fire, that thou mayest be rich; and white raiment, that thou mayest be clothed, and that the shame of thy nakedness do not appear; and anoint thine eyes with eyesalve, that thou mayest see" (Rev. 3:15-18). God calls for a spiritual revival and a spiritual reformation. Unless this takes place, those who are lukewarm will continue to grow more abhorrent to the Lord, until He will refuse to acknowledge them as His children.

A revival and a reformation must take place, under the ministration of the Holy Spirit. Revival and reformation are two different things. Revival signifies a renewal of spiritual life, a quickening of the powers of mind and heart, a resurrection from spiritual death. Reformation signifies a reorganization, a change in ideas and theories, habits and practices. Reformation will not bring forth the good fruit of righteousness unless it is connected with the revival of the Spirit. Revival and reformation are to do their appointed work, and in doing this work they must blend.—*The Review and Herald*, Feb. 25, 1902.

Simple Agencies Will Be Used

Representations have been made to me, showing that the Lord will carry out His plans through a variety of ways and instruments. It is not alone the most talented, not alone those who hold high positions of trust, or are the most highly educated from a worldly point of view, whom the Lord uses to do His grand and holy work of soulsaving. He will use simple means; He will use many who have had few advantages to help in carrying forward His work. He will, by the use of simple means, bring those who possess property and lands to a belief of the truth, and these will be influenced to become the Lord's helping hand in the advancement of His work.—Letter 62, 1909.

Chapter 2:

Conversions— Fake or Real

Power of the Word

Wherever the word of God has been faithfully preached, results have followed that attested its divine origin. The Spirit of God accompanied the message of His servants, and the word was with power. Sinners felt their consciences quickened. The "light which lighteth every man that cometh into the world" illumined the secret chambers of their souls, and the hidden things of darkness were made manifest. Deep conviction took hold upon their minds and hearts. They were convinced of sin and of righteousness and of judgment to come. They had a sense of the righteousness of Jehovah and felt the terror of appearing, in their guilt and uncleanness, before the Searcher of hearts. In anguish they cried out: "Who shall deliver me from the body of this death?" As the cross of Calvary, with its infinite sacrifice for the sins of men, was revealed, they saw that nothing but the merits of Christ could suffice to atone for their transgressions; this alone could reconcile man to God. With faith and humility they accepted the Lamb of God, that taketh away the sin of the world. Through the blood of Jesus they had "remission of sins that are past."

A New Lifestyle

These souls brought forth fruit meet for repentance. They believed and were baptized, and rose to walk in newness of life—new creatures in Christ Jesus; not to fashion themselves according to the former lusts, but by the faith of the Son of God to follow in His steps, to reflect His character, and to purify themselves even as He is pure. The things they once hated they now loved, and the things they once loved they hated. The proud and self-assertive became meek and lowly of heart. The vain and supercilious became serious and unobtrusive. The profane became reverent, the drunken sober, and the profligate pure. The vain fashions of the world were laid aside. Christians sought not the "outward adorning of plaiting the hair, and of wearing of gold, or of putting on of apparel; but . . . the hidden man of the heart, in that which is not corruptible, even the ornament of a meek and quiet spirit, which is in the sight of God of great price" (1 Peter 3:3, 4).

Revivals brought deep heart searching and humility. They were characterized by solemn, earnest appeals to the sinner, by yearning compassion for the purchase of the blood of Christ. Men and women prayed and wrestled with God for the salvation of souls. The fruits of such revivals were seen in souls who shrank not at self-denial and sacrifice, but rejoiced that they were counted worthy to suffer reproach and trial for the sake of Christ. Men beheld a transformation in the lives of those who had professed the name of Jesus. The community was benefited by their influence. . . .

This is the result of the work of the Spirit of God. There is no evidence of genuine repentance unless it works reformation. If he restore the pledge, give again that he had robbed, confess his sins, and love God and his fellow men, the sinner may be sure that he has found peace with God. Such were the effects that in former years followed seasons of religious awakening. Judged by their fruits, they were known to be blessed of God in the salvation of men and the uplifting of humanity.

Counterfeit Revivals—What's the Difference?

But many of the revivals of modern times have presented a marked contrast to those manifestations of divine grace which in earlier days followed the labors of God's servants. It is true that a widespread interest is kindled, many profess conversion, and there are large accessions to the churches; nevertheless the results are not such as to warrant the belief that there has been a corresponding increase of real spiritual life. The light which flames up for a time soon dies out, leaving the darkness more dense than before.

Popular revivals are too often carried by appeals to the imagination, by exciting the emotions, by gratifying the love for what is new and startling. Converts thus gained have little desire to listen to Bible truth, little interest in the testimony of prophets and apostles. Unless a religious service has something of a sensational character, it has no attractions for them. A message which appeals to unimpassioned reason awakens no response. The plain warnings of God's word, relating directly to their eternal interests, are unheeded.

With every truly converted soul the relation to God and to eternal things will be the great topic of life. . . . Before the final visitation of God's judgments upon the earth there will be among the people of the Lord such a revival of primitive godliness as has not been witnessed since apostolic times. The Spirit and power of God will be poured out upon His children. At that time many will separate themselves from those churches in which the love of this world has supplanted love for God and His Word. Many, both of ministers and people, will gladly accept those great truths which God has caused to be proclaimed at this time to prepare a people for the Lord's second coming.

The enemy of souls desires to hinder this work; and before the time for such a movement shall come, he will endeavor to prevent it by introducing a counterfeit. In those churches which he can bring under his deceptive power he will make it appear that God's special blessing is poured out; there will be manifest what is thought to be great religious interest. Multitudes will exult that God is working marvelously for them, when the work is that of another spirit. Under a religious guise, Satan will seek to extend his influence over the Christian world.

Why Be Deceived?

In many of the revivals which have occurred during the last

half century, the same influences have been at work, to a greater or less degree, that will be manifest in the more extensive movements of the future. There is an emotional excitement, a mingling of the true with the false, that is well adapted to mislead. Yet none need be deceived. In the light of God's word it is not difficult to determine the nature of these movements. Wherever men neglect the testimony of the Bible, turning away from those plain, soul-testing truths which require self-denial and renunciation of the world, there we may be sure that God's blessing is not bestowed. And by the rule which Christ Himself has given, "Ye shall know them by their fruits" (Matt. 7:16), it is evident that these movements are not the work of the Spirit of God.

In the truths of His word, God has given to men a revelation of Himself; and to all who accept them they are a shield against the deceptions of Satan. It is a neglect of these truths that has opened the door to the evils which are now becoming so widespread in the religious world. The nature and the importance of the law of God have been, to a great extent, lost sight of. A wrong conception of the character, the perpetuity, and the obligation of the divine law has led to errors in relation to conversion and sanctification, and has resulted in lowering the standard of piety in the church. Here is to be found the secret of the lack of the Spirit and power of God in the revivals of our time. . . .

Can God's Law Be Changed?

Many religious teachers assert that Christ by His death abolished the law, and men are henceforth free from its requirements. There are some who represent it as a grievous yoke, and in contrast to the bondage of the law they present the liberty to be enjoyed under the gospel.

But not so did prophets and apostles regard the holy law of God. Said David: "I will walk at liberty: for I seek Thy precepts" (Ps. 119:45). The apostle James, who wrote after the death of Christ, refers to the Decalogue as "the royal law" and "the perfect law of liberty" (James 2:8; 1:25). And the revelator, half a century after the crucifixion, pronounces a blessing upon them "that do His commandments, that they may have right to the tree of life, and may enter in through the gates into the city" (Rev. 22:14). The claim that Christ by His death abolished His Father's law is without foundation. Had it been possible for the law to be changed or set aside, then Christ need not have died to save man from the penalty of sin. . . .

Alienated and Reconciled—How Does it Happen?

It is the work of conversion and sanctification to reconcile men to God by bringing them into accord with the principles of His law. In the beginning, man was created in the image of God. He was in perfect harmony with the nature and the law of God; the principles of righteousness were written upon his heart. But sin alienated him from his Maker. He no longer reflected the divine image. His heart was at war with the principles of God's law. "The carnal mind is enmity against God: for it is not subject to the law of God, neither indeed can be" (Rom. 8:7). But "God so loved the world, that He gave His only-begotten Son," that man might be reconciled to God. Through the merits of Christ he can be restored to harmony with his Maker. His heart must be renewed by divine grace; he must have a new life from above. This change is the new birth, without which, says Jesus, "he cannot see the kingdom of God."

The first step in reconciliation to God is the conviction of sin. "Sin is the transgression of the law." "By the law is the knowledge of sin" (1 John 3:4; Rom. 3:20). In order to see his guilt, the sinner must test his character by God's great standard of righteousness. It is a mirror which shows the perfection of a righteous character and enables him to discern the defects in his own.

The law reveals to man his sins, but it provides no remedy. While it promises life to the obedient, it declares that death is the portion of the transgressor. The gospel of Christ alone can free him from the condemnation or the defilement of sin. He must exercise repentance toward God, whose law has been transgressed; and faith in Christ, his atoning sacrifice. Thus he obtains "remission of sins that are past" and becomes a partaker of the divine nature. . . .

Is he now free to transgress God's law? Says Paul: "Do we then make void the law through faith? God forbid: yea, we establish the law." "How shall we, that are dead to sin, live any longer therein?" And John declares: "This is the love of God, that we keep His commandments: and His commandments are not grievous" (Rom. 3:31; 6:2; John 5:3). In the new birth the heart is brought into harmony with God, as it is brought into accord with His law. When this mighty change has taken place in the sinner, he has passed from death unto life, from sin unto holiness, from transgression and rebellion to obedience and loyalty. . . .

Sanctification—Who Does the Work?

Erroneous theories of sanctification, . . . springing from neglect or rejection of the divine law, have a prominent place in the religious movements of the day. These theories are both false in doctrine and dangerous in practical results; and the fact that they are so generally finding favor, renders it doubly essential that all have a clear understanding of what the Scriptures teach upon this point.

True sanctification is a Bible doctrine. The apostle Paul, in his letter to the Thessalonian church, declares: "This is the will of God, even your sanctification." And he prays: "The very God of peace sanctify you wholly" (1 Thess. 4:3; 5:23). The Bible clearly teaches what sanctification is and how it is to be attained. The Saviour prayed for His disciples: "Sanctify them through Thy truth: Thy word is truth" (John 17:17, 19). And Paul teaches that believers are to be "sanctified by the Holy Ghost" (Rom. 15:16). What is the work of the Holy Spirit? Jesus told His disciples: "When He, the Spirit of truth, is come, He will guide you into all truth" (John 16:13). And the psalmist says: "Thy law is the truth." By the word and the Spirit of God are opened to men the great principles of righteousness embodied in His law. And since the law of God is "holy, and just, and good," a transcript of the divine perfection, it follows that a character formed by obedience to that law will be holy. Christ is a perfect example of such a character. He says: "I have kept My Father's commandments." "I do always those things that please Him" (John 15:10; 8:29). The followers of Christ are to become like Him—by the grace of God to form characters in harmony with the principles of His holy law. This is Bible sanctification.

This work can be accomplished only through faith in Christ, by the power of the indwelling Spirit of God. Paul admonishes believers: "Work out your own salvation with fear and trembling. For it is God which worketh in you both to will and to do of His good pleasure" (Phil. 2:12, 13). The Christian will feel the promptings of sin, but he will maintain a constant warfare against it. Here is where Christ's help is needed. Human weakness becomes united to divine strength, and faith exclaims: "Thanks be to God, which giveth us the victory through our Lord Jesus Christ" (1 Cor. 15:57).

The Scriptures plainly show that the work of sanctification is progressive. When in conversion the sinner finds peace with God through the blood of the atonement, the Christian life has but just begun. Now he is to "go on unto perfection;" to grow up "unto the measure of the stature of the fullness of Christ." . . . [Phil. 3:13, 14 and 2 Peter 1:5-10 quoted.]

No Room for Boasting

Those who experience the sanctification of the Bible will manifest a spirit of humility. Like Moses, they have had a view of the awful majesty of holiness, and they see their own unworthiness in contrast with the purity and exalted perfection of the Infinite One.

The prophet Daniel was an example of true sanctification. His long life was filled up with noble service for his Master. He was a man "greatly beloved" (Dan. 10:11) of Heaven. Yet instead of claiming to be pure and holy, this honored prophet identified himself with the really sinful of Israel as he pleaded before God in behalf of his people: "We do not present our supplications before Thee for our righteousnesses, but for Thy great mercies." "We have sinned, we have done wickedly." He declares: "I was speaking, and praying, and confessing my sin and the sin of my people. . . ." (Dan. 9:18, 15, 20).

When Job heard the voice of the Lord out of the whirlwind, he exclaimed: "I abhor myself, and repent in dust and ashes" (Job 42:6). It was when Isaiah saw the glory of the Lord, and heard the cherubim crying, "Holy, holy, holy, is the Lord of hosts," that he cried out, "Woe is me! for I am undone" (Isa. 6:3, 5). Paul, after he was caught up into the third heaven and heard things which it was not possible for a man to utter, speaks of himself as "less than the least of all saints" (2 Cor. 12:2-4, margin; Eph. 3:8). It was the beloved John, who leaned on Jesus' breast and beheld His glory, that fell as one dead before the feet of the angel (Rev. 1:17).

There can be no self-exaltation, no boastful claim to freedom from sin, on the part of those who walk in the shadow of Calvary's cross. They feel that it was their sin which caused the agony that broke the heart of the Son of God, and this thought will lead them to self-abasement. Those who live nearest to Jesus discern most clearly the frailty and sinfulness of humanity, and their only hope is in the merit of a crucified and risen Saviour.

Counterfeit Sanctification—Is It "Only Believe"?

The sanctification now gaining prominence in the religious world carries with it a spirit of self-exaltation and a disregard for the law of God that mark it as foreign to the religion of the Bible. Its advocates teach that sanctification is an instantaneous work, by which, through faith alone, they attain to perfect holiness. "Only believe," say they, "and the blessing is yours." No further effort on the part of the receiver is supposed to be required. At the same time they deny the authority of the law of God, urging that they are released from obligation to keep the commandments. But is it possible for men to be holy, in accord with the will and character of

God, without coming into harmony with the principles which are an expression of His nature and will, and which show what is well pleasing to Him?

The desire for an easy religion that requires no striving, no self-denial, no divorce from the follies of the world, has made the doctrine of faith, and faith only, a popular doctrine; but what saith the word of God? Says the apostle James: "What doth it profit, my brethren, though a man say he hath faith, and have not works? can faith save him? . . . Wilt thou know, O vain man, that faith without works is dead? Was not Abraham our father justified by works, when he had offered Isaac his son upon the altar? Seest thou how faith wrought with his works, and by works was faith made perfect? . . . Ye see then how that by works a man is justified, and not by faith only" (James 2:14-24).

The testimony of the word of God is against this ensnaring doctrine of faith without works. It is not faith that claims the favor of Heaven without complying with the conditions upon which mercy is to be granted, it is presumption; for genuine faith has its foundation in the promises and provisions of the Scriptures.

Let none deceive themselves with the belief that they can become holy while willfully violating one of God's requirements. The commission of a known sin silences the witnessing voice of the Spirit and separates the soul from God. . . . Though John in his epistles dwells so fully upon love, yet he does not hesitate to reveal the true character of that class who claim to be sanctified while living in transgression of the law of God. "He that saith, I know Him, and keepeth not His commandments, is a liar, and the truth is not in him. But whoso keepeth His word, in him verily is the love of God perfected" (1 John 2:4, 5). Here is the test of every man's profession. We cannot accord holiness to any man without bringing him to the measurement of God's only standard of holiness in heaven and in earth. . . .

The claim to be without sin is, in itself, evidence that he who makes this claim is far from holy. It is because he has no true conception of the infinite purity and holiness of God or of what they must become who shall be in harmony with His character; because he has no true conception of the purity and exalted loveliness of Jesus, and the malignity and evil of sin, that man can regard himself as holy. The greater the distance between himself and Christ, and the more inadequate his conceptions of the divine character and requirements, the more righteous he appears in his own eyes.

Sanctification—Total Commitment

The sanctification set forth in the Scriptures embraces the entire being—spirit, soul, and body. Paul prayed for the Thessalonians that their "whole spirit and soul and body be preserved blameless unto the coming of our Lord Jesus Christ" (1 Thess. 5:23). Again he writes to believers: "I beseech you therefore, brethren, by the mercies of God, that ye present your bodies a living sacrifice, holy, acceptable unto God" (Rom. 12:1). In the time of ancient Israel every offering brought as a sacrifice to God was carefully examined. If any defect was discovered in the animal presented, it was refused; for God had commanded that the offering be "without blemish." So Christians are bidden to present their bodies, "a living sacrifice, holy, acceptable unto God." In order to do this, all their powers must be preserved in the best possible condition. Every practice that weakens physical or mental strength unfits man for the service of his Creator.

And will God be pleased with anything less than the best we can offer? Said Christ: "Thou shalt love the Lord thy God with all thy heart." Those who do love God with all the heart will desire to give Him the best service of their life, and they will be constantly seeking to bring every power of their being into harmony with the laws that will promote their ability to do His will. . . .

A Changed Life

The world is given up to self-indulgence. "The lust of the flesh, and the lust of the eyes, and the pride of life" control the masses of the people. But Christ's followers have a holier calling. . . .

To those who comply with the conditions, "Come out from among them, and be ye separate, . . . and touch not the unclean," God's promise is, "I will receive you, and will be a Father unto you, and ye shall be My sons and daughters, saith the Lord Almighty" (2 Cor. 6:17, 18). It is the privilege and the duty of every Christian to have a rich and abundant experience in the things of God. . . . The bright beams of the Sun of Righteousness shine upon the servants of God, and they are to reflect His rays. As the stars tell us that there is a great light in heaven with whose glory they are made bright, so Christians are to make it manifest that there is a God on the throne of the universe whose character is worthy of praise and imitation. The graces of His Spirit, the purity and holiness of His character, will be manifest in His witnesses. . . .

No Longer Condemned

While the Christian's life will be characterized by humility, it should not be marked with sadness and self-depreciation. It is the privilege of everyone so to live that God will approve and bless him. It is not the will of our heavenly Father that we should be ever under condemnation and darkness. There is no evidence of true humility in going with the head bowed down and the heart filled with thoughts of self. We may go to Jesus and be cleansed, and stand before the law without shame and remorse. "There is therefore now no condemnation to them which are in Christ Jesus, who walk not after the flesh, but after the Spirit" (Rom. 8:1).

Through Jesus the fallen sons of Adam become "sons of God." "Both He that sanctifieth and they who are sanctified are all of one: for which cause He is not ashamed to call them brethren" (Heb. 2:11). The Christian's life should be one of faith, of victory, and joy in God. "Whatsoever is born of God overcometh the world: and this is the victory that overcometh the world, even our faith" (1 John 5:4). Truly spoke God's servant Nehemiah: "The joy of the Lord is your strength" (Neh. 8:10). And Paul says: "Rejoice in the Lord alway: and again I say, Rejoice." "Rejoice evermore.

Pray without ceasing. In everything give thanks: for this is the will of God in Christ Jesus concerning you" (Phil. 4:4; 1 Thess. 5:16-18).

Such are the fruits of Bible conversion and sanctification.—*The Great Controversy,* pp. 461-478. (Chapter titled "Modern Revivals.")

Chapter 3:

How to Be a
Born-again Christian

Faith—Belief and Trust

When God pardons the sinner, remits the punishment he deserves, and treats him as though he had not sinned, He receives him into divine favor, and justifies him through the merits of Christ's righteousness. The sinner can be justified only through faith in the atonement made through God's dear Son, who became a sacrifice for the sins of the guilty world. No one can be justified by any works of his own. He can be delivered from the guilt of sin, from the condemnation of the law, from the penalty of transgression, only by virtue of the suffering, death, and resurrection of Christ. Faith is the only condition upon which justification can be obtained, and faith includes not only belief but trust. . . .

Many concede that Jesus Christ is the Saviour of the world, but at the same time they hold themselves away from Him, and fail to repent of their sins, fail to accept of Jesus as their personal Saviour. Their faith is simply the assent of the mind and judgment to the truth; but the truth is not brought into the heart, that it might sanctify the soul and transform the character. . . .

Can I Repent Without Help?

Many are confused as to what constitutes the first steps in the work of salvation. Repentance is thought to be a work the sinner must do for himself in order that he may come to Christ. They think that the sinner must procure for himself a fitness in order to obtain the blessing of God's grace. But while it is true that repentance must precede forgiveness, for it is only the broken and contrite heart that is acceptable to God, yet the sinner cannot bring himself to repentance, or prepare himself to come to Christ. Except the sinner repent, he cannot be forgiven; but the question to be decided is as to whether repentance is the work of the sinner or the gift of Christ. Must the sinner wait until he is filled with remorse for his sin before he can come to Christ? The very first step to Christ is taken through the drawing of the Spirit of God; as man responds to this drawing, he advances toward Christ in order that he may repent.

The sinner is represented as a lost sheep, and a lost sheep never returns to the fold unless he is sought after and brought back to the fold by the shepherd. No man of himself can repent, and make himself worthy of the blessing of justification. The Lord Jesus is constantly seeking to impress the sinner's mind and attract him to behold Himself, the Lamb of God, which taketh away the sins of the world. We cannot take a step toward spiritual life save as Jesus draws and strengthens the soul, and leads us to experience that repentance which needeth not to be repented of. . . .

When before the high priests and Sadducees, Peter clearly presented the fact that repentance is the gift of God. Speaking of Christ, he said, "Him hath God exalted with His right hand to be a Prince and a Saviour, for to give repentance to Israel, and forgiveness of sins" (Acts 5:31). Repentance is no less the gift of God than are pardon and justification, and it cannot be experienced except as it is given to the soul by Christ. If we are drawn to Christ, it is through His power and virtue. The grace of contrition comes through Him, and from Him comes justification. . . .

Faith is More Than Talk

The faith that is unto salvation is not a casual faith, it is not the mere consent of the intellect, it is belief rooted in the heart, that embraces Christ as a personal Saviour, assured that He can save unto the uttermost all that come unto God by Him. To believe that He will save others, but will not save you is not genuine faith; but when the soul lays hold upon Christ as the only hope of salvation, then genuine faith is manifested. This faith leads its possessor to place all the affections of the soul upon Christ; his understanding is under the control of the Holy Spirit, and his character is molded after the divine likeness. His faith is not a dead faith, but a faith that works by love, and leads him to behold the beauty of Christ, and to become assimilated to the divine character. . . .

The whole work is the Lord's from the beginning to the end. The perishing sinner may say: "I am a lost sinner; but Christ came to seek and to save that which was lost. He says, 'I came not to call the righteous, but sinners to repentance' (Mark 2:17). I am a sinner, and He died upon Calvary's cross to save me. I need not remain a moment longer unsaved. He died and rose again for my justification, and He will save me now. I accept the forgiveness He has promised."

Righteous in Him

Christ is a risen Saviour; for, though He was dead, He has risen again, and ever liveth to make intercession for us. We are to believe with the heart unto righteousness, and with the mouth make confession unto salvation. Those who are justified by faith will make confession of Christ. "He that heareth My word, and believeth on Him that sent Me, hath everlasting life, and shall not come into condemnation; but is passed from death unto life" (John 5:24). The great work that is wrought for the sinner who is spotted and stained by evil is the work of justification. By Him who speaketh truth he is declared righteous. The Lord imputes unto the believer the righteousness of Christ and pronounces him righteous before the universe. He transfers his sins to Jesus, the sinner's representative, substitute, and surety. Upon Christ He lays the iniquity of every soul that believeth. "He hath made Him to be sin for us, who knew no sin; that we might be made the righteousness of God in Him" (2 Cor. 5:21).

Christ made satisfaction for the guilt of the whole world, and all who will come to God in faith, will receive the righteousness of Christ, "who His own self bare our sins in His own body on the tree, that we, being dead to sins, should live unto righteousness: by whose stripes ye were healed" (1 Peter 2:24). Our sin has been expiated, put away, cast into the depths of the sea. Through repentance and faith we are rid of sin, and look unto the Lord our righteousness. Jesus suffered, the just for the unjust.

What Repentance Is

Although as sinners we are under the condemnation of the law, yet Christ by His obedience rendered to the law, claims for the repentant soul the merit of His own righteousness. In order to obtain the righteousness of Christ, it is necessary for the sinner to know what that repentance is which works a radical change of mind and spirit and action. The work of transformation must begin in the heart, and manifest its power through every faculty of the being; but man is not capable of originating such a repentance as this, and can experience it alone through Christ, who ascended up on high, led captivity captive, and gave gifts unto men.

Who Wants to Repent?

Who is desirous of becoming truly repentant? What must he do? He must come to Jesus, just as he is, without delay. He must believe that the word of Christ is true, and, believing the promise, ask, that he may receive. When sincere desire prompts men to pray, they will not pray in vain. The Lord will fulfill His word, and will give the Holy Spirit to lead to repentance toward God and faith toward our Lord Jesus Christ. He will pray and watch, and put away his sins, making manifest his sincerity by the vigor of his endeavor to obey the commandments of God. With prayer he will mingle faith, and not only believe in but obey the precepts of the law. He will announce himself as on Christ's side of the question. He will renounce all habits and associations that tend to draw the heart from God.

He who would become a child of God must receive the truth that repentance and forgiveness are to be obtained through nothing less than the atonement of Christ. Assured of this the sinner must put forth an effort in harmony with the work done for him, and with unwearied entreaty he must supplicate the throne of grace, that the renovating power of God may come into his soul. Christ pardons none but the penitent, but whom He pardons He first makes penitent. The provision made is complete, and the eternal righteousness of Christ is placed to the account of every believing soul. The costly, spotless robe, woven in the loom of heaven, has been provided for the repenting, believing sinner, and he may say: "I will greatly rejoice in the Lord, my soul shall be joyful in my God; for He hath clothed me with the garments of salvation, He hath covered me with the robe of righteousness" (Isa. 61:10).

Amazing Grace

Abundant grace has been provided that the believing soul may be kept free from sin; for all heaven, with its limitless resources, has been placed at our command. We are to draw from the well of salvation. Christ is the end of law for righteousness to everyone who believeth. In ourselves we are sinners; but in Christ we are righteous. Having made us righteous through the imputed righteousness of Christ, God pronounces us just, and treats us as just. He looks upon us as His dear children. Christ works against the power of sin, and where sin abounded, grace much more abounds. "Therefore being justified by faith, we have peace with God through our Lord Jesus Christ: by whom also we have access by faith into this grace wherein we stand, and rejoice in hope of the glory of God" (Rom. 5:1, 2).

"Being justified freely by His grace through the redemption that is in Christ Jesus: whom God hath set forth to be a propitiation through faith in His blood, to declare His righteousness for the remission of sins that are past, through the forbearance of God; to declare, I say, at this time His righteousness: that He might be just, and the justifier of him which believeth in Jesus" (Rom. 3:24-26). "For by grace are ye saved through faith; and that not of yourselves: it is the gift of God" (Eph. 2:8). [John 1:14-16 quoted.]

Fit to Be Saved

The Lord would have His people sound in the faith—not ignorant of the great salvation so abundantly provided for them. They are not to look forward, thinking that at some future time a great work is to be done for them; for the work is now complete. The believer is not called upon to make his peace with God; he never has nor ever can do this. He is to accept Christ as his peace, for with Christ is God and peace. Christ made an end of sin, bearing its heavy curse in His own body on the tree, and He hath taken away the curse from all those who believe in Him as a personal Saviour. He makes an end of the controlling power of sin in the heart, and the life and character of the believer testify to the genuine character of the grace of Christ.

To those that ask Him, Jesus imparts the Holy Spirit; for it is necessary that every believer should be delivered from pollution, as well as from the curse and condemnation of the law. Through the work of the Holy Spirit, the sanctification of the truth, the believer becomes fitted for the courts of heaven; for Christ works within us, and His righteousness is upon us. Without this no soul will be entitled to heaven. We would not enjoy heaven unless qualified for its holy atmosphere by the influence of the Spirit and the righteousness of Christ.

In order to be candidates for heaven we must meet the requirement of the law: "Thou shalt love the Lord thy God with all thy heart, and with all thy soul, and with all thy strength, and with all thy mind; and thy neighbour as thyself" (Luke 10:27). We can do this only as we grasp by faith the righteousness of Christ. By beholding Jesus we receive a living, expanding principle in the heart, and the Holy Spirit carries on the work, and the believer advances from grace to grace, from strength to strength, from character to character. He conforms to the image of Christ, until in spiritual growth he attains unto the measure of the full stature in Christ Jesus. Thus Christ makes an end of the curse of sin, and sets the believing soul free from its action and effect.

Is There Anything Between Me and God?

Christ alone is able to do this, for "in all things it behoved Him to be made like unto His brethren, that He might be a merciful and faithful high priest in things pertaining to God, to make reconciliation for the sins of the people. For in that He Himself hath suffered being tempted, He is able to succour them that are tempted" (Heb. 2:17, 18). Reconciliation means that every barrier between the soul and God is removed, and that the sinner realizes what the pardoning love of God means. By reason of the sacrifice made by Christ for fallen men, God can justly pardon the transgressor who accepts the merits of Christ. Christ was the channel through which the mercy, love, and righteousness might flow from the heart of God to the heart of the sinner. "He is faithful and just to forgive us our sins, and to cleanse us from all unrighteousness" (1 John 1:9). . . .

Every soul may say: "By His perfect obedience He has satisfied the claims of the law, and my only hope is found in looking to Him as my substitute and surety, who obeyed the law perfectly for me. By faith in His merits I am free from the condemnation of the law. He clothes me with His righteousness, which answers all the demands of the law. I am complete in Him who brings in everlasting righteousness. He presents me to God in the spotless garment of which no thread was woven by any human agent. All is of Christ, and all the glory, honor, and majesty are to be given to the Lamb of God, which taketh away the sins of the world."

Many think that they must wait for a special impulse in order that they may come to Christ; but it is necessary only to come in sincerity of purpose, deciding to accept the offers of mercy and grace that have been extended to us. We are to say: "Christ died to save me. The Lord's desire is that I should be saved, and I will come to Jesus just as I am without delay. I will venture upon the promise. As Christ draws me, I will respond." The apostle says, "With the heart man believeth unto righteousness" (Rom. 10:10). No one can believe with the heart unto righteousness, and obtain justification by faith, while continuing the practice of those things which the Word of God forbids, or while neglecting any known duty.

Good Works the Fruit of Faith

Genuine faith will be manifested in good works; for good works are the fruits of faith. As God works in the heart, and man surrenders his will to God, and cooperates with God, he works out in the life what God works in by the Holy Spirit, and there is harmony between the purpose of the heart and the practice of the life. Every sin must be renounced as the hateful thing that crucified the Lord of life and glory, and the believer must have a progressive experience by continually doing the works of Christ. It is by continual surrender of the will, by continual obedience, that the blessing of justification is retained.

Those who are justified by faith must have a heart to keep the way of the Lord. It is an evidence that a man is not justified by faith when his works do not correspond to his profession. James says, "Seest thou how faith wrought with his works, and by works was his faith made perfect?" (James 2:22).

The faith that does not produce good works does not justify the soul. "Ye see then how that by works a man is justified, and not by faith only" (James 2:24). "Abraham believed God, and it was counted unto him for righteousness" (Rom. 4:3). . . .

In His Steps

Where faith is, good works appear. The sick are visited, the poor are cared for, the fatherless and the widows are not neglected, the naked are clothed, the destitute are fed. Christ went about doing good, and when men are united with Him, they love the children of God, and meekness and truth guide their footsteps. The expression of the countenance reveals their experience, and men take knowledge of them that they have been with Jesus and learned of Him. Christ and the believer become one, and His beauty of character is revealed in those who are vitally connected with the Source of power and love. Christ is the great depositary of justifying righteousness and sanctifying grace.

All may come to Him, and receive of His fullness. He says, "Come unto Me, all ye that labour and are heavy laden, and I will give you rest" (Matt. 11:28). Then why not cast aside all unbelief and heed the words of Jesus? You want rest; you long for peace. Then say from the heart, "Lord Jesus, I come, because Thou hast given me this invitation." Believe in Him with steadfast faith, and He will save you. Have you been looking unto Jesus, who is the author and finisher of your faith? Have you been beholding Him who is full of truth and grace? Have you accepted the peace which Christ alone can give? If you have not, then yield to Him, and through His grace seek for a character that will be noble and elevated. Seek for a constant, resolute, cheerful spirit. Feed on Christ, who is the bread of life, and you will manifest His loveliness of character and spirit.—*Selected Messages*, book 1, pp. 389-398.

Chapter 4:

God Has Rules Too

Our Unique Responsibility

As the Supreme Ruler of the universe, God has ordained laws for the government not only of all living beings, but of all the operations of nature. Everything, whether great or small, animate or inanimate, is under fixed laws which cannot be disregarded. There are no exceptions to this rule; for nothing that the divine hand has made has been forgotten by the divine mind. But while everything in nature is governed by natural law, man alone, as an intelligent being, capable of understanding its requirements, is amenable to moral law. To man alone, the crowning work of His creation, God has given a conscience to realize the sacred claims of the divine law, and a heart capable of loving it as holy, just, and good; and of man prompt and perfect obedience is required. Yet God does not compel him to obey; he is left a free moral agent.

The subject of man's personal responsibility is understood by but few; and yet it is a matter of the greatest importance. We may each obey and live, or we may transgress God's law, defy His authority, and receive the punishment that is meet. Then to every soul the question comes home with force, Shall I obey the voice from heaven, the ten words spoken from Sinai, or shall I go with the multitude who trample on that fiery law? To those who love God it will be the highest delight to keep His commandments, and to do those things that are pleasing in His sight. But the natural heart hates the law of God, and wars against its holy claims. Men shut their souls from the divine light, refusing to walk in it as it shines upon them. They sacrifice purity of heart, the favor of God, and their hope of heaven, for selfish gratification or worldly gain.

Says the psalmist, "The law of the Lord is perfect" (Ps. 19:7). How wonderful in its simplicity, its comprehensiveness and perfection, is the law of Jehovah! It is so brief that we can easily commit every precept to memory, and yet so far-reaching as to express the whole will of God, and to take cognizance, not only of the outward actions, but of the thoughts and intents, the desires and emotions, of the heart. Human laws cannot do this. They can deal with the outward actions only. A man may be a transgressor, and yet conceal his misdeeds from human eyes; he may be a criminal—a thief, a murderer, or an adulterer—but so long as he is not discovered, the law cannot condemn him as guilty. The law of God takes note of the jealousy, envy, hatred, malignity, revenge, lust, and ambition that surge through the soul, but have not found expression in outward action, because the opportunity, not the will, has been wanting. And these sinful emotions will be brought into the account in the day when "God shall bring every work into judgment, with every secret thing, whether it be good, or whether it be evil" (Eccl. 12:14).

Obeying Brings Happiness

The law of God is simple, and easily understood. There are men who proudly boast that they believe only what they can understand, forgetting that there are mysteries in human life and in the manifestation of God's power in the works of nature—mysteries which the deepest philosophy, the most extensive research, is powerless to explain. But there is no mystery in the law of God. All can comprehend the great truths which it embodies. The feeblest intellect can grasp these rules; the most ignorant can regulate the life, and form the character after the divine standard. If the children of men would, to the best of their ability, obey this law, they would gain strength of mind and power of discernment to comprehend still more of God's purposes and plans. And this advancement would be continued, not only during the present life, but during eternal ages; for however far we may advance in the knowledge of

God's wisdom and power, there is always an infinity beyond.

The divine law requires us to love God supremely and our neighbor as ourselves. Without the exercise of this love, the highest profession of faith is mere hypocrisy. . . .

Obedience to the law is essential, not only to our salvation, but to our own happiness and the happiness of all with whom we are connected. "Great peace have they which love Thy law: and nothing shall offend them" (Ps. 119:165), says the Inspired Word. Yet finite man will present to the people this holy, just, and good law, this law of liberty, which the Creator Himself has adapted to the wants of man, as a yoke of bondage, a yoke which no man can bear. But it is the sinner who regards the law as a grievous yoke; it is the transgressor that can see no beauty in its precepts. For the carnal mind "is not subject to the law of God, neither indeed can be" (Rom. 8:7). . . .

Beyond "Thou Shalt Nots"

We are living in an age of great wickedness. Multitudes are enslaved by sinful customs and evil habits, and the fetters that bind them are difficult to break. Iniquity, like a flood, is deluding the earth. Crimes almost too fearful to be mentioned, are of daily occurrence. And yet men professing to be watchmen on the walls of Zion will teach that the law was designed for the Jews only, and passed away with the glorious privileges that ushered in the gospel age. Is there not a relation between the prevailing lawlessness and crime, and the fact that ministers and people hold and teach that the law is no longer of binding force?

The condemning power of the law of God extends, not only to the things we do, but to the things we do not do. We are not to justify ourselves in omitting to do the things that God requires. We must not only cease to do evil, but we must learn to do well. God has given us powers to be exercised in good works; and if these powers are not put to use, we shall certainly be set down as wicked and slothful servants. We may not have committed grievous sins; such offenses may not stand registered against us in the book of

God; but the fact that our deeds are not recorded as pure, good, elevated, and noble, showing that we have not improved our entrusted talents, places us under condemnation.

The law of God existed before man was created. It was adapted to the condition of holy beings; even angels were governed by it. After the Fall, the principles of righteousness were unchanged. Nothing was taken from the law; not one of its holy precepts could be improved. And as it has existed from the beginning, so will it continue to exist throughout the ceaseless ages of eternity. "Concerning Thy testimonies," says the psalmist, "I have known of old that Thou hast founded them for ever" (Ps. 119:152).—*Selected Messages*, book 1, pp. 216-220.

Chapter 5:

The Balance in Faith and Works

A Living Testimony

Without faith it is impossible to please Him; for he that cometh to God must believe that He is, and that He is a rewarder of them that diligently seek Him." There are many in the Christian world who claim that all that is necessary to salvation is to have faith; works are nothing, faith is the only essential. But God's word tells us that faith without works is dead, being alone.

Many refuse to obey God's commandments, yet they make a great deal of faith. But faith must have a foundation. God's promises are all made upon conditions. If we do His will, if we walk in truth, then we may ask what we will, and it shall be done unto us. While we earnestly endeavor to be obedient, God will hear our petitions; but He will not bless us in disobedience. If we choose to disobey His commandments, we may cry, "Faith, faith, only have faith," and the response will come back from the sure word of God, "Faith without works is dead." Such faith will only be as sounding brass and as a tinkling cymbal.

In order to have the benefits of God's grace, we must do our part; we must faithfully work, and bring forth fruits meet for repentance. We are workers together with God. You are not to sit in indolence, waiting for some great occasion, in order to do a great work for the Master. You are not to neglect the duty that lies directly in your pathway; but you are to improve the little opportunities that open around you. You must go on doing your very best in the smaller works of life, taking up heartily and faithfully the work God's providence has assigned you. However small, you should do it with all the thoroughness with which you would do a larger work. Your fidelity will be approved in the records of heaven.

You need not wait for your way to be made smooth before you; go to work to improve your entrusted talents. You have nothing to do with what the world will think of you. Let your words, your spirit, your actions, be a living testimony to Jesus, and the Lord will take care that the testimony for His glory, furnished in a well-ordered life and a godly conversation, shall deepen and intensify in power. Its results may never be seen on earth, but they will be made manifest before God and angels.

What Is My Part?

We are to do all that we can do on our part to fight the good fight of faith. We are to wrestle, to labor, to strive, to agonize to enter in at the strait gate. We are to set the Lord ever before us. With clean hands, with pure hearts, we are to seek to honor God in all our ways. Help has been provided for us in Him who is mighty to save. The spirit of truth and light will quicken and renew us by its mysterious workings; for all our spiritual improvement comes from God, not from ourselves. The true worker will have divine power to aid him, but the idler will not be sustained by the Spirit of God.

In one way we are thrown upon our own energies; we are to strive earnestly to be zealous and to repent, to cleanse our hands and purify our hearts from every defilement; we are to reach the highest standard, believing that God will help us in our efforts. We must seek if we would find, and seek in faith; we must knock, that the door may be opened unto us. The Bible teaches that everything regarding our salvation depends upon our own course of action. If we perish, the responsibility will rest wholly upon ourselves. If provision has been made, and if we accept God's terms, we may lay hold on eternal life. We must come to Christ in faith, we must be diligent to make our calling and election sure.

A Do-nothing Faith?

The forgiveness of sin is promised to him who repents and believes; the crown of life will be the reward of him who is faithful to the end. We may grow in grace by improving through the grace we already have. We are to keep ourselves unspotted from the world, if we would be found blameless in the day of God. Faith and works go hand in hand, they act harmoniously in the work of overcoming. Works without faith are dead, and faith without works is dead. Works will never save us; it is the merit of Christ that will avail in our behalf. Through faith in Him, Christ will make all our imperfect efforts acceptable to God. The faith we are required to have is not a do-nothing faith; saving faith is that which works by love, and purifies the soul. He who will lift up holy hands to God without wrath and doubting, will walk intelligently in the way of God's commandments.

If we are to have pardon for our sins, we must first have a realization of what sin is, that we may repent, and bring forth fruits meet for repentance. We must have a solid foundation for our faith; it must be founded on the Word of God, and its results will be seen in obedience to God's expressed will. Says the apostle, "Without holiness no man shall see the Lord."

Evenly Balanced

Faith and works will keep us evenly balanced, and make us successful in the work of perfecting Christian character. Jesus says, "Not everyone that saith unto Me, Lord, Lord, shall enter into the kingdom of heaven; but he that doeth the will of My Father which is in heaven." Speaking of temporal food, the apostle said, "For even when we were with you, this we commanded you, that if any would not work, neither should he eat." The same rule applies to our spiritual nourishment; if any would have the bread of eternal life, let him make efforts to obtain it.

We are living in an important and interesting period of this earth's history. We need more faith than we have yet had; we need a firmer hold from above. Satan is working with all power to obtain the victory over us, for he knows that he has but a short time in which to work. Paul had fear and trembling in working out his salvation; and should not we fear lest a promise being left us, we should any of us seem to come short of it, and prove ourselves unworthy of eternal life? We should watch unto prayer, strive with agonizing effort to enter in at the strait gate.

There is no excuse for sin, or for indolence. Jesus has led the way, and He wishes us to follow in His steps. He has suffered, He has sacrificed as none of us can, that He might bring salvation within our reach. We need not be discouraged. Jesus came to our world to bring divine power to man, that through His grace, we might be transformed into His likeness.

After My Best—What?

When it is in the heart to obey God, when efforts are put forth to this end, Jesus accepts this disposition and effort as man's best service, and He makes up for the deficiency with His own divine merit. But He will not accept those who claim to have faith in Him, and yet are disloyal to His Father's commandment.

We hear a great deal about faith, but we need to hear a great deal more about works. Many are deceiving their own souls by living an easy-going, accommodating, crossless religion. But Jesus says, "If any man will come after Me, let him deny himself, and take up his cross, and follow Me."—*The Signs of the Times*, June 16, 1890. (Morning talk at Basel, Switzerland, Sept. 17, 1885.)

Like Two Oars

If we are faithful in doing our part, in cooperating with Him, God will work through us [to do] the good pleasure of His will. But God cannot work through us if we make no effort. If we gain eternal life, we must work, and work earnestly. . . . Let us not be deceived by the oft-repeated assertion, "All you have to do is to believe." Faith and works are two oars which we must use equally if we [would] press our way up the stream against the current of unbelief. "Faith, if it hath not works, is dead, being alone." The

Christian is a man of thought and practice. His faith fixes its roots firmly in Christ. By faith and good works he keeps his spirituality strong and healthy, and his spiritual strength increases as he strives to work the works of God.—*Review and Herald*, June 11, 1901.

Present a Balanced Message

Let my brethren be very careful how they present the subject of faith and works before the people, lest minds become confused. . . .

Let no man present the idea that man has little or nothing to do in the great work of overcoming; for God does nothing for man without his cooperation. Neither say that after you have done all you can on your part, Jesus will help you. Christ has said, "Without Me ye can do nothing" (John 15:5). From first to last man is to be a laborer together with God. Unless the Holy Spirit works upon the human heart, at every step we shall stumble and fall. Man's efforts alone are nothing but worthlessness; but cooperation with Christ means a victory. . . .

Never leave the impression on the mind that there is little or nothing to do on the part of man; but rather teach man to cooperate with God, that he may be successful in overcoming.

Let no one say that your works have nothing to do with your rank and position before God. In the judgment the sentence pronounced is according to what has been done or to what has been left undone (Matt. 25:34-40).

Effort and labor are required on the part of the receiver of God's grace; for it is the fruit that makes manifest what is the character of the tree. Although the good works of man are of no more value without faith in Jesus than was the offering of Cain, yet covered with the merit of Christ, they testify [to] the worthiness of the doer to inherit eternal life. That which is considered morality in the world does not reach the divine standard and has no more merit before Heaven than had the offering of Cain.—*Selected Messages*, book 1, pp. 379-382. For a letter to a preacher warning against a one-sided presentation see pages 377-379.

Chapter 6:

Saved Only "In Christ"

"He Will Save Me Now"

The perishing sinner may say: "I am a lost sinner; but Christ came to seek and to save that which was lost. He says, 'I came not to call the righteous, but sinners to repentance' (Mark 2:17). I am a sinner, and He died upon Calvary's cross to save me. I need not remain a moment longer unsaved. He died and rose again for my justification, and He will save me now. I accept the forgiveness He has promised."—*Selected Messages*, book 1, p. 392.

He who repents of his sin and accepts the gift of the life of the Son of God, cannot be overcome. Laying hold by faith of the divine nature, he becomes a child of God. He prays, he believes. When tempted and tried, he claims the power that Christ died to give, and overcomes through His grace. This every sinner needs to understand. He must repent of his sin, he must believe in the power of Christ, and accept that power to save and to keep him from sin. How thankful ought we to be for the gift of Christ's example!—*Ibid.*, p. 224.

Why Worry?

A life in Christ is a life of restfulness. There may be no ecstasy of feeling, but there should be an abiding, peaceful trust. Your hope is not in yourself; it is in Christ. Your weakness is united to His strength, your ignorance to His wisdom, your frailty to His enduring might. . . .

We should not make self the center and indulge anxiety and fear as to whether we shall be saved. All this turns the soul away from the Source of our strength. Commit the keeping of your soul to God, and trust in Him. Talk and think of Jesus. Let self be lost in Him. Put away all doubt; dismiss your fears. Say with the apostle Paul, "I live; yet not I, but Christ liveth in me: and the life which I now live in the flesh I live by the faith of the Son of God, who loved me, and gave Himself for me" (Gal. 2:20). Rest in God. He is able to keep that which you have committed to Him. If you will leave yourself in His hands, He will bring you off more than conqueror through Him that has loved you.—*Steps to Christ*, pp. 70-72.

This You Can Count On

"He who through His own atonement provided for man an infinite fund of moral power, will not fail to employ this power in our behalf. . . . In the whole Satanic force there is not power to overcome one soul who in simple trust casts himself on Christ."—*Christ's Object Lessons*, p. 157.

"Abundant grace has been provided that the believing soul may be kept free from sin."—*Selected Messages*, book 1, p. 394.

"In Him we have a complete offering, an infinite sacrifice, a mighty Saviour, who is able to save unto the uttermost all that come unto God by Him. In love He comes to reveal the Father, to reconcile man to God, to make him a new creature renewed after the image of Him who created him."—*Ibid.*, p. 321.

Peter's Problem

The evil that led to Peter's fall [in denying Christ at His trial] . . . is proving the ruin of thousands today. There is nothing so offensive to God or so dangerous to the human soul as pride and self-sufficiency. Of all sins it is the most hopeless, the most incurable.

Peter's fall was not instantaneous, but gradual. Self-confidence led him to the belief that he was saved, and step after step was taken in the downward path, until he could deny his Master. Never can we safely put confidence in self or feel, this side of heaven, that we are secure against temptation. Those who accept the Saviour, however sincere their conversion, should never be taught to say or to feel that they are saved.*

This is misleading. Every one should be taught to cherish hope and faith; but even when we give ourselves to Christ and know that He accepts us, we are not beyond the reach of temptation. God's Word declares, "Many shall be purified, and made white, and tried" (Dan. 12:10). Only he who endures the trial will receive the crown of life (James 1:12).

Those who accept Christ, and in their first confidence say, I am saved, are in danger of trusting to themselves. They lose sight of their own weakness and their constant need of divine strength. They are unprepared for Satan's devices, and under temptation many, like Peter, fall into the very depths of sin. We are admonished, "Let him that thinketh he standeth, take heed lest he fall" (1 Cor. 10:12). Our only safety is in constant distrust of self, and dependence on Christ.—*Christ's Object Lessons*, pp. 154, 155.

Never Be "Satisfied"

There are many who profess Christ, but who never become mature Christians. They admit that man is fallen, that his faculties are weakened, that he is unfitted for moral achievement, but they say that Christ has borne all the burden, all the suffering, all the self-denial, and they are willing to let Him bear it. They say that there is nothing for them to do but to believe; but Christ said, "If any man will come after Me, let him deny himself, and take up his cross, and follow Me" (Matt. 16:24). Jesus kept the commandments of God. . . .

We are never to rest in a satisfied condition, and cease to make advancement, saying, "I am saved." When this idea is entertained, the motives for watchfulness, for prayer, for earnest endeavor to press onward to higher attainments, cease to exist. No sanctified tongue will be found uttering these words till Christ shall come, and we enter in through the gates into the city of God. Then, with the utmost propriety, we may give glory to God and to the Lamb for eternal deliverance. As long as man is full of weakness—for of himself he cannot save his soul—he should never dare to say, "I am saved."

It is not he that putteth on the armor that can boast of the victory; for he has the battle to fight and the victory to win. It is he that endureth unto the end that shall be saved.—*Selected Messages,* book 1, pp. 313-315.

Connection With Christ—Pretended or Real?

There are both believers and unbelievers in the church. Christ represents these two classes in His parable of the vine and its branches. He exhorts His followers: "Abide in Me, and I in you. As the branch cannot bear fruit of itself, except it abide in the vine; no more can ye, except ye abide in Me. I am the Vine, ye are the branches: He that abideth in Me, and I in him, the same bringeth forth much fruit: for without Me ye can do nothing."

There is a wide difference between a pretended union and a real connection with Christ by faith. A profession of the truth places men in the church, but this does not prove that they have a vital connection with the living Vine. A rule is given by which the true disciple may be distinguished from those who claim to follow Christ but have not faith in Him. The one class are fruit bearing, the other, fruitless. The one are often subjected to the pruning knife of God that they may bring forth more fruit; the other, as withered branches, are erelong to be severed from the living Vine. . . .

The fibers of the branch are almost identical with those of the vine. The communication of life, strength, and fruitfulness from the trunk to the branches is unobstructed and constant. The root sends its nourishment through the branch. Such is the true believer's relation to Christ. He abides in Christ and draws his nourishment from Him.

It's Personal

This spiritual relation can be established only by the exercise of personal faith. This faith must express on our part supreme preference, perfect reliance, entire consecration. Our will must be wholly yielded to the divine will, our feelings, desires, interests, and honor identified with the prosperity of Christ's kingdom and the honor of His cause, we constantly receiving grace from Him, and Christ accepting gratitude from us.

When this intimacy of connection and communion is formed, our sins are laid upon Christ; His righteousness is imputed to us. He was made sin for us that we might be made the righteousness of God in Him. We have access to God through Him; we are accepted in the Beloved. . . .

It was when Christ was about to take leave of His disciples that He gave them the beautiful emblem of His relation to believers. He had been presenting before them the close union with Himself by which they could maintain spiritual life when His visible presence was withdrawn. To impress it upon their minds He gave them the vine as its most striking and appropriate symbol. . . .

All Christ's followers have as deep an interest in this lesson as had the disciples who listened to His words. In the apostasy, man alienated himself from God. The separation is wide and fearful; but Christ has made provision again to connect us with Himself. The power of evil is so identified with human nature that no man can overcome except by union with Christ. Through this union we receive moral and spiritual power. If we have the spirit of Christ we shall bring forth the fruit of righteousness, fruit that will honor and bless men, and glorify God.

The Father is the vinedresser. He skillfully and mercifully prunes every fruit-bearing branch. Those who share Christ's suffering and reproach now will share His glory hereafter. He "is not ashamed to call them brethren." His angels minister to them. His second appearing will be as the Son of man, thus even in His glory identifying Himself with humanity. To those who have united themselves to Him, He declares: "Though a mother may forget her child, 'yet will not I forget thee. Behold, I have graven thee upon the palms of My hands.' Thou art continually before Me."

Pruning the Branches

Oh, what amazing privileges are proffered us!

Will we put forth most earnest efforts to form this alliance with Christ, through which alone these blessings are attained? Will we break off our sins by righteousness and our iniquities by turning unto the Lord? Skepticism and infidelity are widespread. Christ asked the question: "When the Son of man cometh, shall He find faith on the earth?" We must cherish a living, active faith. The permanence of our faith is the condition of our union.

A union with Christ by living faith is enduring; every other union must perish. Christ first chose us, paying an infinite price for our redemption; and the true believer chooses Christ as first and last and best in everything. But this union costs us something. It is a union of utter dependence, to be entered into by a proud being. All who form this union must feel their need of the atoning blood of Christ. They must have a change of heart. They must submit their own will to the will of God. There will be a struggle with outward and internal obstacles. There must be a painful work of detachment as well as a work of attachment. Pride, selfishness, vanity, worldliness—sin in all its forms—must be overcome if we would enter into a union with Christ. The reason why many find the Christian life so deplorably hard, why they are so fickle, so variable, is that they try to attach themselves to Christ without first detaching themselves from these cherished idols.

After the union with Christ has been formed, it can be preserved only by earnest prayer and untiring effort. We must resist, we must deny, we must conquer self. Through the grace of Christ, by courage, by faith, by watchfulness, we may gain the victory.—*Testimonies*, vol. 5, pp. 228-231.

---

* It is the privilege of the Christian to know that on his acceptance of Christ he is saved from his sins and can rejoice in this salvation. But neither the Scriptures nor the Spirit of Prophecy writings supports the popular teaching: "Once saved, always saved." A person may be saved today, but failing to keep his eyes on Jesus and to grow daily in Him, may become self-confident and be lost tomorrow. The apostle Paul declared, "I die daily." In a sense, conversion is a daily experience.

Study carefully the warning drawn from the lesson in Peter's life. Read it in its full context and in conjunction with the similar statement that follows. You will find the perplexing passage to be self-explanatory. Our Lord would have each Christian rejoice freely in his salvation, the salvation he enjoys daily. And when asked, "Are you saved?" he can with assurance answer yes. He will explain that this experience is one that results in constant dependence on God and in daily Christian growth. —White Trustees.

Chapter 7:

Beware
the Counterfeits

This Is The Test

"To the law and to the testimony: if they speak not according to this word, it is because there is no light in them" (Isa. 8:20). The people of God are directed to the Scriptures as their safeguard against the influence of false teachers and the delusive power of spirits of darkness. Satan employs every possible device to prevent men from obtaining a knowledge of the Bible; for its plain utterances reveal his deceptions. At every revival of God's work the prince of evil is aroused to more intense activity; he is now putting forth his utmost efforts for a final struggle against Christ and His followers. The last great delusion is soon to open before us. Antichrist is to perform his marvelous works in our sight. So closely will the counterfeit resemble the true that it will be impossible to distinguish between them except by the Holy Scriptures. By their testimony every statement and every miracle must be tested.—*The Great Controversy*, p. 593.

Why Aren't Miracles Enough?

The man who makes the working of miracles the test of his faith will find that Satan can, through a species of deceptions, perform wonders that will appear to be genuine miracles.—*Selected Messages*, book 2, p. 52.

Satan is a cunning worker, and he will bring in subtle fallacies to darken and confuse the mind and root out the doctrines of salvation. Those who do not accept the Word of God just as it reads, will be snared in his trap.—*Ibid.*

Evil angels are upon our track every moment. . . . They assume new ground and work marvels and miracles in our sight. . . .

Some will be tempted to receive these wonders as from God. The sick will be healed before us. Miracles will be performed in our sight. Are we prepared for the trial which awaits us when the lying wonders of Satan shall be more fully exhibited? Will not many souls be ensnared and taken? By departing from the plain precepts and commandments of God, and giving heed to fables, the minds of many are preparing to receive these lying wonders. We must all now seek to arm ourselves for the contest in which we must soon engage. Faith in God's word, prayerfully studied and practically applied, will be our shield from Satan's power and will bring us off conquerors through the blood of Christ.—*Testimonies*, vol. 1, p. 302.

Healing Can Be From the Devil

I am instructed to say that in the future great watchfulness will be needed. There is to be among God's people no spiritual stupidity. Evil spirits are actively engaged in seeking to control the minds of human beings. Men are binding up in bundles, ready to be consumed by the fires of the last days. Those who discard Christ and His righteousness will accept the sophistry that is flooding the world. Christians are to be sober and vigilant, steadfastly resisting their adversary the devil, who is going about as a roaring lion, seeking whom he may devour. Men under the influence of evil spirits will work miracles. . . .

We need not be deceived. Wonderful scenes, with which Satan will be closely connected, will soon take place. God's Word declares that Satan will work miracles. He will make people sick, and then will suddenly remove from them his satanic power. They will then be regarded as healed. These works of apparent healing will bring Seventh-day Adventists to the test. Many who have had great light will fail to walk in the light, because they have not become one with Christ.—*Selected Messages*, book 2, p. 53.

If those through whom cures are performed, are disposed, on

account of these manifestations, to excuse their neglect of the law of God, and continue in disobedience, though they have power to any and every extent, it does not follow that they have the great power of God. On the contrary, it is the miracle-working power of the great deceiver. He is a transgressor of the moral law, and employs every device that he can master to blind men to its true character. We are warned that in the last days he will work with signs and lying wonders. And he will continue these wonders until the close of probation, that he may point to them as evidence that he is an angel of light and not of darkness.— *Ibid.* pp. 50, 51.

False "Tongues" Identified in 1864

A spirit of fanaticism has ruled a certain class of Sabbathkeepers there; they have sipped but lightly at the fountain of truth and are unacquainted with the spirit of the message of the third angel. . . .

Some of these persons have exercises which they call gifts and say that the Lord has placed them in the church. They have an unmeaning gibberish which they call the unknown tongue, which is unknown not only by man but by the Lord and all heaven. Such gifts are manufactured by men and women, aided by the great deceiver. Fanaticism, false excitement, false talking in tongues, and noisy exercises have been considered gifts which God has placed in the church. Some have been deceived here. . . .

Fanaticism and noise have been considered special evidences of faith. Some are not satisfied with a meeting unless they have a powerful and happy time. They work for this and get up an excitement of feeling.

But the influence of such meetings is not beneficial. When the happy flight of feeling is gone, they sink lower than before the meeting because their happiness did not come from the right source. The most profitable meetings for spiritual advancement are those which are characterized with solemnity and deep searching of heart; each seeking to know himself, and earnestly, and in deep humility, seeking to learn of Christ. . . .

There are wandering stars professing to be ministers sent of God who are preaching the Sabbath from place to place, but who have truth mixed up with error and are throwing out their mass of discordant views to the people. Satan has pushed them in to disgust intelligent and sensible unbelievers. Some of these have much to say upon the gifts and are often especially exercised. They give themselves up to wild, excitable feelings and make unintelligible sounds which they call the gift of tongues, and a certain class seem to be charmed with these strange manifestations. A strange spirit rules with this class, which would bear down and run over anyone who would reprove them. God's Spirit is not in the work and does not attend such workmen. They have another spirit.—*Testimonies*, vol. 1, pp. 411-414.

The world will not be converted by the gift of tongues, or by the working of miracles, but by preaching Christ crucified.—*Testimonies to Ministers*, p. 424.

Drums, Dancing, and Noise

The things you have described as taking place in Indiana,[1] the Lord has shown me would take place just before the close of probation. Every uncouth thing will be demonstrated. There will be shouting, with drums, music, and dancing. The senses of rational beings will become so confused that they cannot be trusted to make right decisions. And this is called the moving of the Holy Spirit.

The Holy Spirit never reveals itself in such methods, in such a bedlam of noise. This is an invention of Satan to cover up his ingenious methods for making of none effect the pure, sincere, elevating, ennobling, sanctifying truth for this time. . . . A bedlam of noise shocks the senses and perverts that which if conducted aright might be a blessing. The powers of Satanic agencies blend with the din and noise, to have a carnival, and this is termed the Holy Spirit's working. . . . Those participating in the supposed revival receive impressions which lead them adrift. They cannot tell what they formerly knew regarding Bible principles.

Bodies Out of Control

No encouragement should be given to this kind of worship. The same kind of influence came in after the passing of the time in 1844. The same kind of representations were made. Men became excited, and were worked by a power thought to be the power of God. They turned their bodies over and over, like a carriage wheel, claiming that they could not do this except by supernatural power. There was a belief that the dead were raised and had ascended to heaven. The Lord gave me a message for this fanaticism; for the beautiful principles of Bible truth were being eclipsed.

Nudity

Men and women, supposed to be guided by the Holy Spirit, held meetings in a state of nudity. They talked about holy flesh. They said they were beyond the power of temptation, and they sang, and shouted, and made all manner of noisy demonstrations. These men and women were not bad, but they were deceived and deluded. . . . Satan was moulding the work, and sensuality was the result. The cause of God was dishonored. Truth, sacred truth, was leveled in the dust by human agencies.

The authorities of the land interfered, and several of the ring leaders were incarcerated within prison walls. By those who were confined in prison this interference was termed persecution for the truth's sake, and thus truth was clothed with garments spotted with the flesh. . . . I presented the reproof of the Lord regarding this kind of work, showing that its influence was making the truth objectionable and disgusting to the community. . . .

I bore my testimony, declaring that these fanatical movements, this din and noise, were inspired by the spirit of Satan, who was working miracles to deceive if possible the very elect.—Letter 132, 1900. (Portions in *Selected Messages*, book 2, pp. 36, 37.)

Confusion

We need to be on our guard, to maintain a close connection with Christ, that we be not deceived by Satan's devices. The Lord desires to have in His service order and discipline, not excitement and confusion.—*Selected Messages*, book 2, p. 35.

Wild, clamorous cries and exercises are no evidence that the Spirit of God is at work.—*Review and Herald*, March 5, 1889.

Order Versus Impressions and Feelings

There are many restless spirits who will not submit to discipline, system, and order. They think that their liberties would be abridged were they to lay aside their own judgment and submit to the judgment of those of experience. The work of God will not progress unless there is a disposition to submit to order and expel the reckless, disorderly spirit of fanaticism from their meetings.

Impressions and feelings are no sure evidence that a person is led by the Lord. Satan will, if he is unsuspected, give feelings and impressions. These are not safe guides. All should thoroughly acquaint themselves with the evidences of our faith, and the great study should be how they can adorn their profession and bear fruit to the glory of God.—*Testimonies*, vol. 1, p. 413.

Satan's Slaves

On every side, Satan seeks to entice the youth into the path of perdition; and if he can once get their feet set in the way, he hurries them on in their downward course, leading them from one dissipation to another, until his victims lose their tenderness of conscience, and have no more the fear of God before their eyes. They exercise less and less self-restraint. They become addicted to the use of wine and alcohol, tobacco and opium,[2] and go from one stage of debasement to another. They are slaves to appetite. Counsel which they once respected, they learn to despise. They put on swaggering airs, and boast of liberty when they are the slaves to selfishness, debased appetite, and licentiousness.—*Temperance*, p. 274.

"Inspired" By Drugs

For some time he [a patient at the Battle Creek Sanitarium]

had thought he was obtaining new light. He was very ill, and must soon die. . . . Those to whom he presented his views listened to him eagerly, and some thought him inspired. . . . To many his reasoning seemed to be without a flaw. They told of his powerful exhortations in his sickroom. Most wonderful views passed before him. But what was the source of his inspiration? It was the morphine[3] given him to relieve his pain.—*Selected Messages*, book 2, p. 113.

Pantheism, Spiritualism, and Free Love

The theory that God is an essence pervading all nature is one of Satan's most subtle devices. It misrepresents God and is a dishonor to His greatness and majesty. Pantheistic theories are not sustained by the Word of God. . . . They gratify the natural heart and give license to inclination.—*Testimonies*, vol. 8, p. 291.

The theory that God is an essence pervading all nature is received by many who profess to believe the Scriptures; but, however beautifully clothed, this theory is a most dangerous deception. It misrepresents God and is a dishonor to His greatness and majesty. And it surely tends not only to mislead, but to debase men. Darkness is its element, sensuality its sphere. . . . These theories, followed to their logical conclusion, sweep away the whole Christian economy. They do away with the necessity for the atonement and make man his own savior.—*The Ministry of Healing*, pp. 428, 429.

I have seen the results of these fanciful views of God, in apostasy, spiritualism, and free-lovism. The free love tendency of these teachings was so concealed that at first it was difficult to make plain its real character. Until the Lord presented it to me, I knew not what to call it, but I was instructed to call it unholy spiritual love.—*Testimonies*, vol. 8, p. 292.

As in the days of the apostles men tried by tradition and philosophy to destroy faith in the Scriptures, so today, by the pleasing sentiments of higher criticism, evolution, spiritualism, theosophy, and pantheism, the enemy of righteousness is seeking to lead souls into forbidden paths. . . . By spiritualism, multitudes are taught to believe that desire is the highest law, that license is liberty, and that man is accountable only to himself.—*The Acts of the Apostles*, p. 474.

Irrational Behavior

Sanctification is not a happy flight of feeling, not the work of an instant, but the work of a lifetime. If any one claims that the Lord has sanctified him, and made him holy, the proof of his claim to the blessing will be seen in the fruits of meekness, patience, long-suffering, truthfulness, and love.

If the blessing that those who claim to be sanctified have received, leads them to rely upon some particular emotion, and they declare there is no need of searching the Scriptures that they may know God's revealed will, then the supposed blessing is a counterfeit, for it leads its possessors to place value on their own unsanctified emotions and fancies, and to close their ears to the voice of God in His word. . . .

Nervous excitement in religious matters is no evidence that the Spirit of God is working upon the heart. We read of frenzied contortions of the body, of shrieking and screaming in the work of Satan upon the minds and bodies of men; but the word of God affords us no example of any such manifestations in connection with those upon whom He pours out His Spirit. It is clear that distempered fancies, wild outbursts, and contorted bodily exercises are the workings of the enemy.

Yet many think that the disorder of the mind, which is intensified by the power of Satan, is a warrant that God is causing these deceived souls to act in so uncomely a manner. The whole spirit and tone of the Bible condemns men in acting without reason or intelligence. When the Spirit of God moves upon the heart, it causes the faithful, obedient child of God to act in a manner that will commend religion to the good judgment of sensible-minded men and women.—*Signs of the Times*, Feb. 28, 1895.

Pretending

Said Christ: "Not every one that saith unto Me, Lord, Lord, shall enter into the kingdom of heaven; but he that doeth the will of My Father which is in heaven. Many will say to Me in that day, Lord, Lord, have we not prophesied in Thy name? and in Thy name have cast out devils? and in Thy name done many wonderful works? And then will I profess unto them, I never knew you: depart from Me, ye that work iniquity."

These may profess to be followers of Christ, but they have lost sight of their Leader. They may say, "Lord, Lord"; they may point to the sick who are healed through them, and to other marvelous works, and claim that they have more of the Spirit and power of God than is manifested by those who keep His law. But their works are done under the supervision of the enemy of righteousness, whose aim it is to deceive souls, and are designed to lead away from obedience, truth, and duty.

In the near future there will be still more marked manifestations of this miracle-working power; for it is said of him, "And he doeth great wonders, so that he maketh fire come down from heaven on the earth in the sight of men."

We are surprised to see so many ready to accept these great pretensions as the genuine work of the Spirit of God; but those who look to wonderful works merely, and are guided by impulse and impressions, will be deceived. . . .

Claims to Holiness

No one who claims holiness is really holy. Those who are registered as holy in the books of Heaven are not aware of the fact, and are the last ones to boast of their own goodness. None of the prophets and apostles ever professed holiness, not even Daniel, Paul, or John. The righteous never make such a claim.

The more nearly they resemble Christ, the more they lament their unlikeness to Him; for their consciences are sensitive, and they regard sin more as God regards it. They have exalted views of God and of the great plan of salvation; and their hearts, humbled under a sense of their own unworthiness, are alive to the honor of being accounted members of the royal family, sons and daughters of the King Eternal.

Those who love the law of God cannot harmonize in worship or in spirit with the determined transgressors of that law, who are filled with bitterness and malice when the plainly revealed truths of the Bible are taught. We have a detector which discriminates between the true and the false. "To the law and to the testimony: if they speak not according to this word, it is because there is no light in them."—*Ibid.*, Feb. 26, 1885.

Whose Voice Can I Trust?

We need to be anchored in Christ, rooted and grounded in the faith. Satan works through agents. He selects those who have not been drinking of the living waters, whose souls are athirst for something new and strange, and who are ever ready to drink at any fountain that may present itself. Voices will be heard, saying, "Lo, here is Christ," or "Lo, there"; but we must believe them not. We have unmistakable evidence of the voice of the True Shepherd, and He is calling upon us to follow Him. He says, "I have kept My Father's commandments." He leads His sheep in the path of humble obedience to the law of God, but He never encourages them in the transgression of that law.

"The voice of a stranger" is the voice of one who neither respects nor obeys God's holy, just, and good law. Many make great pretensions to holiness, and boast of the wonders they perform in healing the sick, when they do not regard this great standard of righteousness. But through whose power are these cures wrought? Are the eyes of either party opened to their transgressions of the law? and do they take their stand as humble, obedient children, ready to obey all of God's requirements? . . .

None need be deceived. The law of God is as sacred as His throne, and by it every man who cometh into the world is to be judged. There is no other standard by which to test character. "If they speak not according to this word, it is because there is no light in them." Now shall the case be decided according to the Word of God, or shall man's pretensions be credited? Christ says, "By their fruits ye shall know them."—*Selected Messages*, book 2, p. 50.

---

[1] Reference is here made to the "Holy Flesh" movement of 1900-1901. See Selected Messages, book 2, pp. 31-39.—White Trustees.

[2] The source of morphine is opium. A fast-working derivative of morphine is heroin.

[3] The source of morphine is opium. A fast-working derivative of morphine is heroin.

Chapter 8:

It's Still a Fight

What Sin Has Done

More clearly than we do we need to understand the issues at stake in the great conflict in which we are engaged. We need to understand more fully the value of the truths of the word of God and the danger of allowing our minds to be diverted from them by the great deceiver.

The infinite value of the sacrifice required for our redemption reveals the fact that sin is a tremendous evil. Through sin the whole human organism is deranged, the mind is perverted, the imagination corrupted. Sin has degraded the faculties of the soul. Temptations from without find an answering chord within the heart, and the feet turn imperceptibly toward evil.

As the sacrifice in our behalf was complete, so our restoration from the defilement of sin is to be complete. No act of wickedness will the law of God excuse; no unrighteousness can escape its condemnation. The ethics of the gospel acknowledge no standard but the perfection of the divine character. . . .

It Takes Perseverance

Wrongs cannot be righted, nor can reformations in conduct be made by a few feeble, intermittent efforts. Character building is the work, not of a day, nor of a year, but of a lifetime. The struggle for conquest over self, for holiness and heaven, is a lifelong struggle. Without continual effort and constant activity, there can be no advancement in the divine life, no attainment of the victor's crown.

The strongest evidence of man's fall from a higher state is the fact that it costs so much to return. The way of return can be gained only by hard fighting, inch by inch, hour by hour. In one moment, by a hasty, unguarded act, we may place ourselves in the power of evil; but it requires more than a moment to break the fetters and attain to a holier life. The purpose may be formed, the work begun; but its accomplishment will require toil, time, perseverance, patience, and sacrifice.

We cannot allow ourselves to act from impulse. We cannot be off guard for a moment. Beset with temptations without number, we must resist firmly or be conquered. Should we come to the close of life with our work undone, it would be an eternal loss.

The life of the apostle Paul was a constant conflict with self. He said, "I die daily" (1 Cor. 15:31). His will and his desires every day conflicted with duty and the will of God. Instead of following inclination, he did God's will, however crucifying to his nature.

At the close of his life of conflict, looking back over its struggles and triumphs, he could say, "I have fought a good fight, I have finished my course, I have kept the faith: henceforth there is laid up for me a crown of righteousness, which the Lord, the righteous Judge, shall give me at that day" (2 Tim. 4:7, 8).

The Christian life is a battle and a march. In this warfare there is no release; the effort must be continuous and persevering. It is by unceasing endeavor that we maintain the victory over the temptations of Satan. Christian integrity must be sought with resistless energy and maintained with a resolute fixedness of purpose.

No one will be borne upward without stern, persevering effort in his own behalf. All must engage in this warfare for themselves; no one else can fight our battles. . . .

There's a Science to It

There is a science of Christianity to be mastered—a science as much deeper, broader, higher than any human science as the heavens are higher than the earth. The mind is to be disciplined, educated, trained; for we are to do service for God in ways that are not in harmony with inborn inclination. Hereditary and cultivated tendencies to evil must be overcome. Often the education and training of a lifetime must be discarded, that one may become a learner in the school of Christ. Our hearts must be educated to become steadfast in God. We are to form habits of thought that will enable us to resist temptation. We must learn to look upward. The principles of the word of God—principles that are as high as heaven, and that compass eternity—we are to understand in their bearing upon our daily life. Every act, every word, every thought, is to be in accord with these principles. All must be brought into harmony with, and subject to, Christ.

The precious graces of the Holy Spirit are not developed in a moment. Courage, fortitude, meekness, faith, unwavering trust in God's power to save, are acquired by the experience of years. By a life of holy endeavor and firm adherence to the right the children of God are to seal their destiny.

No Time to Lose

We have no time to lose. We know not how soon our probation may close. At the longest, we have but a brief lifetime here, and we know not how soon the arrow of death may strike our hearts. We know not how soon we may be called to give up the world and all its interests. Eternity stretches before us. The curtain is about to be lifted. But a few short years, and for everyone now numbered with the living the mandate will go forth:

"He that is unjust, let him be unjust still: . . . and he that is righteous, let him be righteous still: and he that is holy, let him be holy still" (Rev. 22:11).

Are we prepared? Have we become acquainted with God, the Governor of heaven, the Lawgiver, and with Jesus Christ whom He sent into the world as His representative? When our lifework is ended, shall we be able to say, as did Christ our example:

"I have glorified Thee on the earth: I have finished the work which Thou gavest Me to do. . . . I have manifested Thy name"? John 17:4-6.

The angels of God are seeking to attract us from ourselves and from earthly things. Let them not labor in vain.

Minds that have been given up to loose thought need to change. "Gird up the loins of your mind, be sober, and hope to the end for the grace that is to be brought unto you at the revelation of Jesus Christ; as obedient children, not fashioning yourselves according to the former lusts in your ignorance: but as He which hath called you is holy, so be ye holy in all manner of conversation; because it is written, Be ye holy; for I am holy" (1 Peter 1:13-16).

The thoughts must be centered upon God. We must put forth earnest effort to overcome the evil tendencies of the natural heart. Our efforts, our self-denial and perseverance, must be proportionate to the infinite value of the object of which we are in pursuit. Only by overcoming as Christ overcame shall we win the crown of life.

Constant Dependence

Man's great danger is in being self-deceived, indulging self-sufficiency, and thus separating from God, the source of his strength. Our natural tendencies, unless corrected by the Holy Spirit of God, have in them the seeds of moral death. Unless we become vitally connected with God, we cannot resist the unhallowed effects of self-indulgence, self-love, and temptation to sin.

In order to receive help from Christ, we must realize our need. We must have a true knowledge of ourselves. It is only he who knows himself to be a sinner that Christ can save. Only as we see our utter helplessness and renounce all self-trust, shall we lay hold on divine power.

It is not only at the beginning of the Christian life that this renunciation of self is to be made. At every advance step heavenward it is to be renewed. All our good works are dependent on a power outside of ourselves; therefore there needs to be a continual reaching out of the heart after God, a constant, earnest confession of sin and humbling of the soul before Him. Perils surround us; and we are safe only as we feel our weakness and cling with the grasp of faith to our mighty Deliverer.

Truth or Trivia

We must turn away from a thousand topics that invite attention. There are matters that consume time and arouse inquiry, but end in nothing. The highest interests demand the close attention and energy that are so often given to comparatively insignificant things.

Accepting new theories does not in itself bring new life to the soul. Even an acquaintance with facts and theories important in themselves is of little value unless put to a practical use. We need to feel our responsibility to give our souls food that will nourish and stimulate spiritual life. . . .

The question for us to study is, "What is truth—the truth that is to be cherished, loved, honored, and obeyed?" The devotees of science have been defeated and disheartened in their efforts to find out God. What they need to inquire at this time is, "What is the truth that will enable us to win the salvation of our souls?"

Do I Have the Answer?

"What think ye of Christ?"—this is the all-important question. Do you receive Him as a personal Saviour? To all who receive Him He gives power to become sons of God.

Christ revealed God to His disciples in a way that performed in their hearts a special work, such as He desires to do in our hearts. There are many who, in dwelling too largely upon theory, have lost sight of the living power of the Saviour's example. They have lost sight of Him as the humble, self-denying worker. What they need is to behold Jesus. Daily we need the fresh revealing of His presence. We need to follow more closely His example of self-renunciation and self-sacrifice.

We need the experience that Paul had when he wrote: "I am crucified with Christ: nevertheless I live; yet not I, but Christ liveth in me: and the life which I now live in the flesh I live by the faith of the Son of God, who loved me, and gave Himself for me" (Gal. 2:20).

The knowledge of God and of Jesus Christ expressed in character is an exaltation above everything else that is esteemed on earth or in heaven. It is the very highest education. It is the key that opens the portals of the heavenly city. This knowledge it is God's purpose that all who put on Christ shall possess.—*The Ministry of Healing*, pp. 451-457.

Chapter 9:

Safeguarding the New Experience

The Contest Following the Revival[1]

After the outpouring of the Spirit of God in Battle Creek it was proved in the college that a time of great spiritual light is also a time of corresponding spiritual darkness. Satan and his legions of satanic agencies are on the ground, pressing their powers upon every soul to make of none effect the showers of grace that have come from heaven to revive and quicken the dormant energies into decided action to impart that which God has imparted. Had all the many souls, then enlightened, gone to work at once to impart to others that which God had given to them for that very purpose, more light would have been given, more power bestowed. God does not give light merely for one person but that he may diffuse light, and God be glorified. Its influence is felt.

In every age seasons of spiritual revival and the outpouring of the Holy Spirit have been followed by spiritual darkness and prevailing corruptions. Taking into account that which God has done in opportunities and privileges and blessings in Battle Creek, the church has not made honorable progress in doing her work, and God's blessing will not rest upon the church in advancing still more light until they use the light as God has directed in His Word. The light that would shine in clear and distinct rays will grow dim amid the moral darkness. The aggressive power of the truth of God is dependent upon the cooperation of the human agent with God in piety, in zeal, in unselfish efforts to get the light of truth before others.—Manuscript 45, 1893.

Peril of Confusing the Spirit's Work with Fanaticism

There have been things written to me in regard to the movings of the Spirit of God at the last conference (1893), and at the college, which clearly indicate that because these blessings were not lived up to, minds have been confused, and that which was light from heaven has been called excitement. I have been made sad to have this matter viewed in this light. We must be very careful not to grieve the Holy Spirit of God, in pronouncing the ministration of His Holy Spirit a species of fanaticism. How shall we understand the workings of the Spirit of God if it was not revealed in clear and unmistakable lines, not only in Battle Creek but in many places?

I am not surprised that anyone should be confused at the after result. But in my experience of the past forty-nine years I have seen much of these things, and I have known that God has wrought in a marked manner; and let no one venture to say this is not the Spirit of God. It is just that which we are authorized to believe and pray for, for God is more willing to give the Holy Spirit to them that ask Him than parents are to give good gifts unto their children. But the Holy Spirit is not for the human agent to work; it is to work and use the human agent. That God did abundantly bless the students in the school and the church, I have not one doubt; but a period of great light and the outpouring of the Spirit is quite generally followed by a time of great darkness. Why? Because the enemy works with all his deceiving energies to make of none effect the deep movings of the Spirit of God on the human subject.

When the students at the school went into their match games and football playing, when they became absorbed in the amusement question, Satan saw it a good time to step in and make of none effect the Holy Spirit of God in molding and using the human subject. Had the teachers to a man done their duty, had they realized their accountability, had they stood in moral independence before God, had they used the ability which God had given them according to the sanctification of the spirit through the love of the truth, they would have had spiritual strength and divine enlightenment to press on and on and upward on the ladder of progress reaching heavenward. The fact is evident that they did not appreciate or walk in the light or follow the Light of the world.

It is an easy matter to idle away, talk and play away, the Holy Spirit's influence. To walk in the light is to keep moving onward in the direction of light. If the one blessed becomes negligent and inattentive and does not watch unto prayer, if he does not lift the cross and bear the yoke of Christ, if his love of amusements and strivings for the mastery absorb his power or ability, then God is not made the first and best and last in everything, and Satan comes in to act his part in playing the game of life for his soul. He can play much more earnestly than they can play, and make deep-laid plots for the ruin of the soul. . . .

The results after the working of the Spirit of God in Battle Creek are not because of fanaticism, but because those who were blessed did not show forth the praises of Him who called them out of darkness into His marvelous light; and when the earth is lightened with the glory of God, some will not know what it is, and from whence it came, because they misapplied and misinterpreted the Spirit shed upon them. God is a jealous God of His own glory. He will not honor those who dishonor Him. Some persons living in the light ought to have instructed these souls young in experience to walk in the light after they had received the light. I wish I had time to write more fully, but I fear I have not.—Letter 58, 1893.

Easy Ways to Lose the Blessing

Some things have been urged upon my mind with great force of late, and I feel constrained by the Spirit of God to write in reference to them.[2] Has the Lord graciously opened to you the windows of heaven and poured you out a blessing? Oh! Then, that was the very time to educate the teachers and students how to retain the precious favor of God by working in accordance with increased light, and send its precious rays to others. Has Heaven's light been given? And for what purpose has it been given? That the light should shine forth in practical works of righteousness. When those so abundantly blessed shall be seen with deeper and more fervent piety, having a sense that they have been bought with the precious blood of the Lamb of God, and are clothed with the garments of His salvation, will they not represent Christ?

Have not the playing of games, and rewards, and the using of the boxing glove been educating and training after Satan's direction to lead to the possession of his attributes? What if they could see Jesus, the Man of Calvary looking upon them in sorrow, as was represented to me. Things are certainly receiving a wrong mold, and are counteracting the work of the divine power which has been graciously bestowed. The work of every true Christian is to represent Christ, to reflect light, to elevate the standard of morals, and by words and influence consecrated to God, to compel the careless and reckless to think of God and eternity. The world would gladly drop eternity out of their reckoning, but they cannot succeed so long as there are those who represent Christ in their practical life.

Every believer forms a link in the golden chain connecting the soul to Jesus Christ, and is the channel of communication of that light to those who are in darkness. Let one lose his connection with Christ, and Satan seizes the opportunity to lead him to dishonor Christ by words, by spirit, by action, and thus Christ's character is misinterpreted. I ask you, my brother, if the religion of Jesus Christ is not by the excess of the amusements misunderstood. When the Lord gave to Battle Creek the riches of His grace, were there those in responsibility who could have directed these souls as to how to improve upon the endowment given, in doing good, useful work that would give a change from their studies, other than the excitement and emotions caused by their games? This kind of pastime is not improving mind or spirit or manners for the preparation for the scenes of trial that they must soon enter. The superficial piety that passes for religion will be consumed when tried in the furnace.

The Lord would have the teachers consider the contagion of their own example. They need to pray much more and consider that the convictions which flow out from a well-ordered life and a godly conversation, from a living, decided Christianity, are the preparation of the garden of the heart for the seeds of truth to be planted for a fruitful harvest, and for the Sun of Righteousness when He comes with healing in His beams. Let your righteousness so shine before men, "that they may see your good works, and glorify your Father which is in heaven" (Matt. 5:16). "Ye are," said Christ to His disciples, "the salt of the earth: but if the salt have lost his savour, wherewith shall it be salted? it is thenceforth good for nothing, but to be cast out, and to be trodden under foot of men" (Matt. 5:13). The church illuminates the world, not by their profession of godliness, but by their manifestation of the transforming, sanctifying power of the truth on life and character. . . .

The time is altogether too full of tokens of the coming conflict to be educating the youth in fun and games.—Letter 46, 1893.

Danger of Light Becoming Darkness

The Lord has condescended to give you an outpouring of His Holy Spirit. At the camp meetings, and in our various institutions, a great blessing has been showered upon you. You have been visited by the heavenly messengers of light and truth and power, and it should not be thought a strange thing that God should thus bless you. How does Christ subdue His chosen people to Himself? It is by the power of His Holy Spirit; for the Holy Spirit, through the Scriptures, speaks to the mind, and impresses truth upon the hearts of men. Before His crucifixion, Christ promised that the Comforter should be sent to His disciples. He said: "It is expedient for you that I go away: for if I go not away, the Comforter will not come unto you; but if I depart, I will send him unto you. And when he is come, he will reprove the world of sin, and of righteousness, and of judgment. . . . When he, the Spirit of truth, is come, he will guide you into all truth: for he shall not speak of himself; but whatsoever he shall hear, that shall he speak: and he will shew you things to come. He shall glorify me: for he shall receive of mine, and shall shew it unto you" (John 16:7, 8, 13-15).

This promise of Christ has been made little enough of, and because of a dearth of the Spirit of God, the spirituality of the law and its eternal obligations have not been comprehended. Those who have professed to love Christ, have not comprehended the relation which exists between them and God, and it is still but dimly outlined to their understanding. They but vaguely comprehend the amazing grace of God in giving His only-begotten Son for the salvation of the world. They do not understand how far reaching are the claims of the holy law, how intimately the precepts of the law are to be brought into practical life. They do not realize what a great privilege and necessity are prayer, repentance, and the doing of the words of Christ. It is the office of the Holy Spirit to reveal to the mind the character of the consecration that God will accept. Through the agency of the Holy Spirit, the soul is enlightened, and the character is renewed, sanctified, and uplifted.

Through the deep movings of the Spirit of God, I have had opened before me the character of the work of the visitation of the Spirit of God. I have had opened before me the danger in which souls would be placed who had been thus visited; for afterward, they would have to meet fiercer assaults of the enemy, who would press upon them his temptations to make of none effect the workings of the Spirit of God, and cause that the momentous truths presented and witnessed by the Holy Spirit, should not purify and sanctify those who had received the light of heaven, and thus cause that Christ should not be glorified in them.

The period of great spiritual light, if that light is not sacredly cherished and acted upon, will be turned into a time of corresponding spiritual darkness. The impression made by the Spirit of God, if men do not cherish the sacred impression, and occupy holy ground, will fade from the mind. Those who would advance in spiritual knowledge must stand by the very fount of God, and drink again and again from the wells of salvation so graciously opened unto them. They must never leave the source of refreshment; but with hearts swelling with gratitude and love at the display of the goodness and compassion of God, they must be continually partakers of the living water.

Oh, how much this means to every soul—"I am the light of the world"; "I am the bread of life: he that cometh to me shall never hunger (for anything more satisfying); and he that believeth on me shall never thirst" (John 8:12; 6:35). To come to this condition means that you have found the Source of light and love, and have learned when and how you may be replenished, and may make use of the promises of God by continually applying them to your souls.

"But I said unto you, That ye also have seen me, and believe not" (John 6:36). This has been literally fulfilled in the cases of many; for the Lord gave them a deeper insight into truth, into His character of mercy and compassion and love; and yet after being thus enlightened, they have turned from Him in unbelief. They saw the deep movings of the Spirit of God; but when the insidious temptations of Satan came in, as they always will come after a season of revival, they did not resist unto blood, striving against sin; and those who might have stood on vantage ground, had they made a right use of the precious enlightenment that they had, were overcome by the enemy. They should have reflected the light that God gave to them upon the souls of others; they should have worked and acted in harmony with the sacred revealings of the Holy Spirit; and in not doing so, they suffered loss.

Spiritual Victory Lost to the Passions for Games

Among the students the spirit of fun and frolic was indulged. They became so interested in playing games that the Lord was crowded out of their minds; and Jesus stood among you in the playground, saying, O that thou hadst known, "even thou, at least in this thy day, the things which belong unto thy peace!" (Luke 19:42). "Ye also have seen me, and believe not" (John 6:36). Yes; Christ revealed Himself to you, and deep impressions were made as the Holy Spirit moved upon your hearts; but you pursued a course by which you lost these sacred impressions, and failed to maintain the victory. "All that the Father giveth me shall come to me; and him that cometh to me I will in no wise cast out" (John 6:37). You began to come to Christ, but you did not abide in Christ. You forsook Him, and the realization you had had of the great favors and blessings He had given you, was lost from your heart. The question of amusement occupied so large a place in your minds, that after the solemn visitation of the Spirit of God, you entered into its discussion with such great zeal that all barriers were broken down; and through your passion for games, you neglected to heed the word of Christ: "Watch ye and pray, lest ye enter into temptation" (Mark 14:38). The place that should have been occupied by Jesus was usurped by your passion for games. You chose your amusements instead of the comfort of the Holy Spirit. You did not follow the example of Jesus, who said, "I came down from heaven, not to do mine own will, but the will of him that sent me" (John 6:38).

The minds of many are so bewildered with their own human desires and inclinations, and they have been so in the habit of indulging them, that they cannot comprehend the true sense of the Scriptures. Many suppose that in following Christ they will be obliged to be gloomy and disconsolate, because they are required to deny themselves the pleasures and follies that the world indulge in. The living Christian will be filled with cheerfulness and peace, because he lives as seeing Him who is invisible; and those who seek Christ in His true character have within them the elements of everlasting life, because they are partakers of the divine nature, having escaped the corruptions that are in the world through lust. Jesus said, "This is the Father's will which hath sent me, that of all which he hath given me, I should lose nothing, but should raise it up again at the last day. And this is the will of him that sent me, that every one which seeth the Son, and believeth on him, may have everlasting life: and I will raise him up at the last day" (John 6:39, 40).

The Child of God a Laborer With God

All spiritual life is derived from Jesus Christ. "As many as received him, to them gave he power to become the sons of God"

(John 1:12). But what is the sure result of becoming a child of God? The result is that we become laborers together with God. There is a great work to be done for your own soul's salvation, and to qualify you to win others from unbelief to a life sustained by faith in Christ Jesus: "Verily, verily, I say unto you, He that believeth on me (with a casual faith?—No, with an abiding faith that works by love and purifies the soul) hath everlasting life. I am that bread of life. . . . I am the living bread which came down from heaven: if any man eat of this bread, he shall live for ever: and the bread that I will give is my flesh, which I will give for the life of the world. . . . Except ye eat the flesh of the Son of man, and drink his blood, ye have no life in you. Whoso eateth my flesh, and drinketh my blood, hath eternal life; and I will raise him up at the last day. . . . It is the Spirit that quickeneth; the flesh profiteth nothing: the words that I speak unto you, they are spirit, and they are life. But there are some of you that believe not. For Jesus knew from the beginning who they were that believed not, and who should betray him. And he said, Therefore said I unto you, that no man can come unto me, except it were given unto him of my Father" (John 6:47, 48, 51, 53, 54, 63-65).

When Jesus spoke these words, He spoke them with authority, assurance, and power. At times He manifested Himself in such a way that the deep movings of His Spirit were sensibly realized. But many who saw and heard and participated in the blessings of the hour, went their way, and soon forgot the light He had given them.

The treasures of eternity have been committed to the keeping of Jesus Christ, to give to whomsoever He will; but how sad it is that so many quickly lose sight of the precious grace that is proffered unto them through faith in Him. He will impart the heavenly treasures to those who will believe in Him, look to Him, and abide in Him. He thought it not robbery to be equal with God, and He knows no restraint nor control in bestowing the heavenly treasures upon whom He will. He does not exalt and honor the great ones of the world, who are flattered and applauded; but He calls upon His chosen, peculiar people who love and serve Him, to come unto

Him and ask, and He will give them the bread of life, and endow them with the water of life, which shall be in them as a well of water springing up unto everlasting life.

Jesus brought to our world the accumulated treasures of God, and all who believe upon Him are adopted as His heirs. He declares that great shall be the reward of them who suffer for His name's sake, It is written, "Eye hath not seen, nor ear heard, neither have entered into the heart of man, the things which God hath prepared for them that love him" (1 Cor. 2:9).—*The Review and Herald*, Jan. 30, 1894.

Was the Blessing Cherished?

In order to increase our spiritual endowment, it is necessary to walk in the light. In view of the event of Christ's soon coming, we must be vigilantly working to prepare our own souls, to keep our own lamps trimmed and burning, and to urge upon others the necessity of getting ready for the coming of the Bridegroom. Watching and working must go together; faith and works must be united, or our characters will not be symmetrical and well-balanced, perfect in Christ Jesus.

Should we give our lives up to prayerful meditation, our lights would grow dim, for light is given to us that we may impart it to others, and the more we impart light, the brighter our own light will become. If there is any one thing in the world in which we may manifest enthusiasm, it may be manifested in seeking the salvation of the souls for whom Christ died. Work of this kind will not cause us to neglect personal piety. The exhortation is given for us to be "not slothful in business; fervent in spirit; serving the Lord" (Rom. 12:11).

To have an eye single to the glory of God means to have singleness of purpose, to show forth the work that has been wrought in your heart, that subdues your will to the will of God, and brings into captivity every thought to the glory of God. The world has been looking upon you to see what would be the afterinfluence of the work of revival that came to the college, the sanitarium, the office of publication, and to the members of the church in Battle Creek. What testimony have you borne in your daily life and character?

God expected you all to do your best, not to please, amuse, and glorify yourselves, but to honor Him in all your ways, returning unto Him according to the light and privileges that He had given you through the endowment of His grace. He expected you to testify before heavenly intelligences, and to be living witnesses to the world, of the power of the grace of Christ. The Lord tested you, to see if you would treat His rich blessing as a cheap, light matter, or regard it as a rich treasure to be handled with reverent awe. If all had treated the gift of God in this manner—for the work was of God—then, according to the measure of each one's responsibility, the grace given would have been doubled, as were the talents of him who traded diligently with his lord's money.

A Blessing Turned Into a Curse

God has been testing the fidelity of His people, proving them to see what use they would make of His intrusted precious blessing. This blessing came from our Intercessor and Advocate in the heavenly courts; but Satan was ready to enter any avenue that was open for him, in order that he might turn the light and blessing into darkness and cursing.

How may the blessing be turned into a curse? By persuading the human agent not to cherish the light, or not to reveal to the world that it has been effective in transforming the character. Imbued with the Holy Spirit, the human agent consecrates himself to cooperate with divine agencies. He bears the yoke of Christ, lifts his burdens, and works in Christ's line to gain precious victories. He walks in the light as Christ is in the light. The scripture is fulfilled to him, "We all, with open face beholding as in a glass the glory of the Lord, are changed into the same image from glory to glory even as by the Spirit of the Lord" (2 Cor. 3:18).

Another year has now passed into eternity with its burden of record; and the light which shone from heaven upon you was to prepare you to arise and shine, to show forth the praises of God to the world as His commandment-keeping people. You were to be living witnesses; but if no special endeavor of a high and holy character bears testimony before the world, if no higher effort has been made than that which is seen in the popular churches of the day, then the name of God has not been honored, and His truth has not been magnified before the world, by presenting divine credentials in the people who have received great light. If they have had no greater appreciation of the manifest power of God than to eat and drink, and rise up to play, as did ancient Israel, then how can the Lord trust His people with rich and gracious manifestations? If they act directly contrary in almost every respect to the known will of God, and are found in carelessness, in levity, in selfishness, in ambition and pride, corrupting their way before the Lord, how can He give them another outpouring of the Holy Spirit?

God has the richest blessing for His people; but He cannot bestow it until they know how to treat the precious gift in showing forth the praises of Him who has called them out of darkness into His marvelous light. "Wherefore seeing we also are compassed about with so great a cloud of witnesses, let us lay aside every weight, and the sin which doth so easily beset us, and let us run with patience the race that is set before us, looking unto Jesus the author and finisher of our faith; who for the joy that was set before him endured the cross, despising the shame, and is set down at the right hand of the throne of God" (Heb. 12:1, 2). A portion of the joy which was set before Christ, was the joy of seeing His truth armed with the omnipotent power of the Holy Spirit, impressing His image upon the life and character of His followers.

Divine intelligences cooperate with human agencies as they seek to magnify the law and make it honorable. The law of the Lord is perfect, converting the soul. It is in the converted soul that the world sees a living testimony. Then shall the Lord of heaven have room to work? Shall He find a place in the hearts of those who claim to believe the truth? Shall His pure, disinterested benevolence meet with a response from the human agent? Shall the world see a display of the glory of Christ in the characters of those who profess to be His disciples? Shall Christ be favored and glorified in seeing His own sympathy and love pouring forth in streams of goodness and truth from His human agents? In implanting His gospel in the heart, He is pouring out the resources of heaven for the blessing of the world. "We are labourers together with God: ye are God's husbandry, ye are God's building" (1 Cor. 3:9).

What has the rich blessing of God done for those who were humble and contrite in heart to receive it? Has the blessing been cherished? Have the receivers been showing forth the praises of Him who has called them out of darkness into His marvelous light? There are some who are already questioning the work that was so good, and that should have been most highly appreciated. They are looking upon it as a certain species of fanaticism.

Be Exceedingly Careful

It would be surprising if there were not some, who, not being well-balanced in mind, have spoken and acted indiscreetly; for whenever and wherever the Lord works in giving a genuine blessing, a counterfeit is also revealed, in order to make of none effect the true work of God. Therefore we need to be exceedingly careful, and walk humbly before God, that we may have spiritual eyesalve that we may distinguish the working of the Holy Spirit of God from the working of that spirit that would bring in wild license and fanaticism. "By their fruits ye shall know them" (Matt. 7:20). Those who are really beholding Christ will be changed into His image, even by the Spirit of the Lord, and will grow up to the full stature of men and women in Christ Jesus. The Holy Spirit of God will inspire men with love and purity; and refinement will be manifest in their characters.

But because some have misappropriated the rich blessing of

heaven, shall others deny that Jesus, the Saviour of the world, has passed through our churches, and that to bless? Let not doubt and unbelief question this; for in so doing, you are treading on dangerous ground. God has given the Holy Spirit to those who have opened the door of their hearts to receive the heavenly gift. But let them not yield to the temptation afterward to believe that they have been deceived. Let them not say, "Because I feel darkness, and am oppressed with doubt, and never saw Satan's power so manifest as now, therefore I was mistaken." I warn you to be careful. Sow not one expression of doubt. God has wrought for you, bringing sound doctrines of truth into actual contact with the heart. Blessing was given you, that it might produce fruit in sound practices and upright character.

The Sin of Rejecting Evidence

The sin for which Christ reproved Chorazin and Bethsaida was the sin of rejecting evidence that would have convinced them of the truth, had they yielded to its power. The sin of the scribes and Pharisees was the sin of placing the heavenly work which had been wrought before them in the darkness of unbelief, so that the evidence which should have led them into a settled faith was questioned, and the sacred things which should have been cherished were regarded as of no value. I fear that the people have permitted the enemy to work along these very lines, so that the good which emanated from God, the rich blessing which He has given, have come to be regarded by some as fanaticism.

If this attitude is preserved, then when the Lord shall again let His light shine upon the people, they will turn from the heavenly illumination, saying, "I felt the same in 1893, and some in whom I have had confidence, said that the work was fanaticism." Will not those who have received the rich grace of God, and who take the position that the working of the Holy Spirit was fanaticism, be ready to denounce the operations of the Spirit of God in the future, and the heart thus be proof against the solicitations of the still, small voice? The love of Jesus may be presented to those who thus barricade themselves against it, and exercise no constraining power upon them. The riches of the grace of heaven may be bestowed and yet rejected, instead of being cherished and gratefully recognized. With the heart men did believe unto righteousness, and for a time confession was made unto salvation; but, sad to relate, the receiver did not cooperate with heavenly intelligences, and cherish the light by working the works of righteousness.—*The Review and Herald*, Feb. 6, 1894.

---

[1] In 1893 there was a marked revival in our institutions at our Battle Creek headquarters, with large evidence of the work of the Spirit of God. Much of the blessing was lost in events which followed in quick succession. In this experience and the counsel given in connection with it may be found lessons which are of value today.—Compilers.

[2] Addressed to the president of Battle Creek College.

Chapter 10:

Special Appeals in Public Ministry[1]

At Battle Creek in Early Days

Attended meeting at the church at Battle Creek. Spoke to the people about one hour with freedom, in regard to the fall of Adam bringing misery and death, Christ bringing life and immortality to light through His humiliation and death. Felt to urge upon the people the necessity of entire consecration to God—the sanctification of the entire being, soul, body, and spirit. Spoke upon the death of Moses and the view he had of the promised land of Canaan. There was a depth of feeling in the congregation. . . . In meeting that evening we called those forward who had a desire to be Christians. Thirteen came forward. All bore testimony for the Lord. It was a good work.—Diary, Jan. 12, 1868.

Earnest Work at Tittabawassee, Michigan

Meetings were held all through the day. My husband spoke in forenoon; Brother Andrews in the afternoon. I followed with remarks quite at length, entreating those who had been interested through the meetings to commence from that day to serve God. We called forward those who wished to start in the service of the Lord. Quite a number came forward. I spoke several times, beseeching souls to break the bands of Satan and start then. One mother went to her son and wept and entreated him. He seemed hard, stubborn, and unyielding. I then arose and addressed Brother D, begged him to not stand in the way of his children. He started, then arose, spoke, said he would commence from that day. This was heard with glad hearts by all. Brother D is a precious man.

Sister E's husband then arose, testified that he would be a Christian. He is an influential man—a lawyer. His daughter was upon the anxious seat. Brother D then added his entreaties to ours. Sister D's also to their children. We entreated and at last prevailed. All came forward. The fathers and all the sons and other fathers followed their example. It was a day of gladness. Sister E said it was the happiest day of her life.—Diary, Feb. 19, 1868.

A Good Response in Battle Creek

I spoke in the afternoon from 2 Peter. I had freedom in talking. After I had spoken one hour I invited those who wished to be Christians to come forward. Between thirty and forty came forward quietly without excitement and occupied the front seats. I spoke with them in regard to making an entire surrender to God. We had a praying season for those who came forward. We had a very precious season of prayer. Those who wished baptism were requested to signify it by rising. Quite a number arose.—Diary, June 9, 1873.

After Some Hesitancy a Response

I spoke in the afternoon [at Stanley, Va.] from John 17:3. The Lord gave me much of His Holy Spirit. The house was full. I called those forward who wished to seek the Lord more earnestly and for those who wished to give themselves to the Lord a whole sacrifice. For a time not one made a move, but after a while many came forward and bore testimonies of confession. We had a precious season of prayer and all felt broken down, weeping and confessing their sins. O that each may understand!—Diary, Nov. 9, 1890.

As She Begins Work in Switzerland

Sabbath and Sunday were precious seasons.[2] The Lord especially blessed (me) in speaking Sunday afternoon. At the close of the discourse an invitation was given for all who desired to be Christians, and all who felt that they had not a living connection with God, to come forward, that we might unite our prayers with theirs for the pardon of sin, and for grace to resist temptation.

This was a new experience for many, but they did not hesitate. It seemed that the entire congregation were on their feet, and the best they could do was to be seated, and all seek the Lord together. Here was an entire congregation manifesting their determination to put away sin, and to engage most earnestly in the work of seeking God. After prayer, one hundred and fifteen testimonies were borne. Many of these showed a genuine experience in the things of God.—*Historical Sketches of the Foreign Missions of the Seventh-day Adventists*, p. 173.

At Christiana [Oslo], Norway

We spent two weeks in Christiana, and labored earnestly for the church. The Spirit of the Lord moved me to bear a very plain testimony. At our last meeting especially, I presented before them the necessity of a thorough change in the character if they would be children of God. . . . I urged upon them the necessity of deep repentance, confession, and forsaking of the sins which had shut away the sweet spirit of Christ from the church. We then called for those to come forward who would take a decided position on the Lord's side. Many responded. Some good confessions were made, and earnest testimonies were borne.—*The Review and Herald*, Oct. 19, 1886.

Determination Indicated by Standing

A request was made [at Basel, Switzerland] for all who would from this time make most earnest efforts to reach a higher standard to arise. All arose. We hope this now will have the effect to win them to God and to heavenly reflections and make earnest efforts to be all that God has given them power to be—faithful and true devoted soldiers of the cross of Christ.—*Diary*, Nov. 22, 1885.

Backsliders Reclaimed in Basel

In the afternoon of the Sabbath we assembled again for social meeting. The blessing of the Lord rested upon me as I again addressed the people for a short time. Every seat was full and extra seats were brought in. All listened with deep interest.

I invited those who desired the prayers of the servants of God to come forward. All who had been backslidden, all who wished to return to the Lord and seek Him diligently, could improve the opportunity. Several seats were quickly filled and the whole congregation was on the move. We told them the best they could do was to be seated right where they were and we would all seek the Lord together by confessing our sins, and the Lord had pledged His word, "If we confess our sins, he is faithful and just to forgive us our sins, and to cleanse us from all unrighteousness" (1 John 1:9).

Many testimonies were borne in quick succession and with depth of feelings, showing that the hearts were touched by the Spirit of God. Our meetings continued from two o'clock P.M. to five, and then we were obliged to close, with several earnest prayers.—Diary, Feb. 20, 1887.

An Outstanding Experience in Australia

On Sabbath, May 25 [1895], we had a precious meeting in the hall where our people meet at North Fitzroy. For several days before the meeting, I knew that I was expected to speak in the church on Sabbath; but unfortunately I had a severe cold and was quite hoarse. I felt inclined to excuse myself from this appointment; but as it was my only opportunity, I said, "I will place myself before the people, and I believe the Lord will answer my earnest prayers, and remove the hoarseness so that I can present my message to the people." I presented to my heavenly Father the promise, "Ask, and it shall be given you; seek, and ye shall find; knock, and it shall be opened unto you. For every one that asketh receiveth; and he that seeketh findeth; and to him that knocketh it shall be opened. . . . If ye, then, being evil, know how to give good gifts unto your children: how much more shall your heavenly Father give the Holy Spirit to them that ask him?" (Luke 11:9-13). . . .

The word of God is sure. I had asked, and I believed that I would be enabled to speak to the people. I selected a portion of

Scripture; but when I rose to speak, it was taken from my mind, and I felt impressed to speak from the first chapter of second Peter. The Lord gave me special freedom in presenting the value of the grace of God. . . . I was enabled by the aid of the Holy Spirit to speak with clearness and power.

At the close of my discourse, I felt impressed by the Spirit of God to extend an invitation for all those to come forward who desired to give themselves fully to the Lord. Those who felt the need of the prayers of the servants of God were invited to make it manifest. About thirty came forward. Among those were the wives of the Brethren F, who for the first time made manifest their desire to come near to God. My heart was filled with unspeakable gratitude because of the movement made by these two women.

I could then see why I was so earnestly moved to make this invitation. At first I had hesitated, wondering if it were best to do so when my son and I were the only ones whom I could see who would give us any help on that occasion. But as though someone had spoken to me, the thought passed through my mind, "Cannot you trust in the Lord?" I said, "I will, Lord." Although my son was much surprised that I should make such a call on this occasion, he was equal to the emergency. I never heard him speak with greater power or deeper feeling than at this time. He called upon Brethren Faulkhead and Salisbury to come forward, and we knelt in prayer. My son took the lead, and the Lord surely indited his petition; for he seemed to pray as though in the presence of God. Brethren Faulkhead and Salisbury also presented fervent petitions, and then the Lord gave me a voice to pray. I remembered the Sisters F, who, for the first time, were taking a public stand for the truth. The Holy Spirit was in the meeting, and many were stirred by its deep movings.

At the close of the meeting many pressed their way to the platform, and taking me by the hand, requested me with tears in their eyes to pray for them. I answered heartily, "I will." The Sisters F were introduced to me, and I found that their hearts were very tender. . . . The mother of one of the sisters who has now taken her position on the truth, has been a most bitter opposer, and has threatened that if her daughter did become a Sabbathkeeper, she would not allow her to enter her home; for the mother would look upon her as a disgrace to the family. Mrs. F had often made the statement that she would never join the Seventh-day Adventists. She had been brought up in the Presbyterian Church, and had been educated to think that it was very improper for women to speak in meeting, and that for a woman to preach was altogether beyond the bounds of propriety. She enjoyed hearing Elders Daniells and Corliss, and thought them very clever speakers, but she would not listen to a woman's preaching. Her husband had prayed that God would so arrange matters that she might be converted under the ministry of Sister White. When I made the appeal, and urged those to come forward who felt their need of drawing nearer to God, to the surprise of all, these sisters came forward. The sister who had lost her little one, said that she was determined that she would not move forward, but the Spirit of the Lord so forcibly impressed her mind that she dared not refuse. . . . I feel so grateful to my heavenly Father for His lovingkindness in bringing these two precious souls to unite with their husbands in obeying the truth.—*The Review and Herald*, July 30, 1895.

Non-Adventist Visitors Respond at Ashfield Church

I invited all who wanted to give themselves to God in a sacred covenant, and to serve Him with their whole hearts, to rise to their feet. The house was full, and nearly all rose. Quite a number not of our faith were present, and some of these arose. I presented them to the Lord in earnest prayer, and we know that we had the manifestation of the Spirit of God. We felt that a victory had indeed been gained.—Manuscript 30a, 1896.

The Special Call at the Battle Creek College

I have now spoken to the helpers, nursing class, and physicians five times during the Week of Prayer, and I am sure my talks are appreciated. I have spoken in the college twice. Last Thursday

Professor Prescott wished me to come over there. I went and prayed and spoke to the large chapel filled with students. I had much freedom in speaking and in presenting before them the goodness and mercy of God and the great condescension and sacrifice of Jesus Christ and the heavenly reward purchased for us, the last final victory, and what a privilege it is to be Christians.

Professor Prescott arose and attempted to speak, but his heart was full and he did not utter a word for five minutes, but stood weeping before the people. Then he said a few words, "I am glad that I am a Christian." He talked for about five minutes, then he gave liberty for all to speak. Many testimonies were borne, but it seemed to me that there must be a company reached that we had not yet succeeded in reaching. We called all to come forward who felt that they were unready for Christ's coming and had not an evidence of their acceptance with God. I thought the whole house was in motion. We then gave opportunity for all to express their feelings, but we had after a little another season of prayer and the blessing of the Lord seemed to reach hearts.

Then we separated into divisions and continued the work for two hours longer, and the Lord's Spirit came into the meeting in a remarkable manner. Several of those who had known nothing of a religious faith, unbelievers from the world, have obtained a genuine experience in the religious life. And the work is going deeper and deeper. The Lord is at work and will work, as fast as we prepare the way for Him that He can safely reveal His power in our behalf. — Letter 75, 1888.

Called Forward in San Francisco

Friday, December 21 (1900), I went to San Francisco, where I was to spend the Week of Prayer. Sabbath afternoon I spoke to the church there, although I was so weak that I had to cling to the pulpit with both hands to steady myself. I asked the Lord to give me strength to speak to the people. He heard my prayer, and strengthened me. I had great freedom in speaking from Rev. 2:1-5.

The deep moving of the Spirit of God came upon me, and the

people were strongly impressed with the message borne. After I had finished speaking, all who desired to give themselves to the Lord were invited to come forward. A large number responded, and prayer was offered for them. Several who came forward are persons who have recently heard the Advent message, and are in the valley of decision. May the Lord strengthen the good impression made upon them, and may they give themselves wholly to Him. Oh, how I long to see souls converted, and hear them sing a new song, even praise to our God!

Sunday afternoon I spoke to a large audience, many of whom are not of our faith. My strength was renewed, and I was able, without clinging to the desk, to stand before the people. The Lord's blessing rested upon us, and increased strength came to me as I spoke. As on Sabbath, those seeking spiritual help were invited to come forward, and we were glad to see the ready response. The Lord came very near as we sought Him in prayer.—*The Review and Herald*, Feb. 19, 1901.

A Similar Work in Every Church

Sabbath, November 10, I visited San Francisco, and spoke to a church full of people who had ears to hear and hearts to understand. . . . After I had finished speaking, Elder Corliss invited all who wished to give themselves to Jesus to come forward. There was a quick and happy response, and I was told that nearly two hundred persons came forward. Men and women, youth and children, pressed into the front seats. The Lord would be pleased to have a work similar to this done in every church.

Many could not come forward, because the house was so crowded, yet the animated countenances and tearful eyes testified to the determination, "I will be on the Lord's side. From this time I will seek earnestly to reach a higher standard."—*The Review and Herald*, Feb. 12, 1901.

Response at General Conference of 1909

My brethren and sisters, seek the Lord while He may be found.

There is a time coming when those who have wasted their time and opportunities will wish they had sought Him. . . . He wants you to keep in the line of reason, and in the line of labor. He wants you to go forth to our churches to labor earnestly for Him. He wants you to institute meetings for those outside of the churches, that they may learn the truths of this last message of warning. There are places where you will be gladly received, where souls will thank you for coming to their help. May the Lord help you to take hold of this work as you have never yet taken hold of it. Will you do this? Will you here rise to your feet and testify that you will make God your trust and your helper? [Congregation rises.]

[Praying] I thank thee, Lord God of Israel. Accept this pledge of this Thy people. Put Thy Spirit upon them. Let Thy glory be seen in them. As they shall speak the word of truth, let us see the salvation of God. Amen.—*General Conference Bulletin*, May 18, 1909.

---

[1] Ellen G. White, in her public ministry effectively employed the appeal which called for a response. Presented here are accounts of a number of instances which reveal her use of such methods under varying circumstances.—Compilers.

[2] At the Swiss conference held in Basel, Switzerland, in 1885.